EDUCATION FOR LADIES

Education for Ladies
1830-1860

IDEAS ON EDUCATION
IN MAGAZINES FOR WOMEN

Eleanor Wolf Thompson

KING'S CROWN PRESS
Morningside Heights · New York
1947

KING'S CROWN PRESS

*is a division of Columbia University Press organized for the purpose
of making certain scholarly material available at minimum cost.
Toward that end, the publishers have adopted every reasonable
economy except such as would interfere with a legible format.
The work is presented substantially as submitted by the author,
without the usual editorial attention of Columbia University Press.*

HMS

Foreword

To SEEK ideas on education in the magazines for ladies of a century ago may at first seem absurd. Yet tucked away among love stories, "poems" reeking with sentimentality, "cards" of advertisement, news items, "receipts," and book reviews are descriptions of schools, comments on curricula, discussions of the aims of education, and pertinent remarks upon that much debated question of whether woman had a mind capable of thought. In fact, through advertisements, schools for young ladies and at times for young gentlemen were presented to their mothers. Every editor "clipped" or "copied" news and comments about developments in education. Discussions of the aims of education were popular alike both for "fillers" and for editorials. Phases of education were celebrated in poetry. A teacher was even a suitable heroine. The "sphere" of woman and the "proper" education for it provided springboards for innumerable discussions. Education was a vital topic in the magazines for ladies. *Mrs. Stephens' Illustrated Monthly Magazine* was the only mid-nineteenth century ladies' magazine that has been found which did not present ideas on education to its readers. Because education loomed importantly in the magazines for ladies of a century ago, this study has been made.

In some respects, this study has grown circuitously. At first the plan was to use "education" in the larger sense, the sense in which the editors themselves used it, when they referred to their magazines as "educational projects." The editors, however, presented ideas on such a multiplicity of subjects that it soon became apparent that so broad a conception of the meaning of "education" would result in a social history of the period. Consequently education was limited to a professional usage.

As the connotation of education was narrowed, so the conception

of magazines for ladies was broadened to include magazines which
ladies might have read, as well as those published primarily for them.
In addition to forty magazines for ladies, thirty-seven general magazines, two American magazines published in French and nine in
German have been read. These magazines have been selected to
represent varying interests, different shades of opinion and all sections of the country. In addition, ten educational journals have been
consulted in order to compare the ideas on education accepted by the
educators of the day with those presented to the laity.

The period 1830–1860 has been chosen for a number of reasons.
It was a period of great growth in periodical literature. Publishers
were eager to satisfy the awakened interests of the common man,
who was becoming increasingly convinced of his rights and of the
equality of all men. As the common woman drove an entering wedge
into his domain, publishers sent forth in growing numbers their
ventures in magazines for ladies. Since there was little paid advertising, the survival of the periodicals depended upon the readers.
Magazines, therefore, presented ideas acceptable to ordinary men
and women.

The period 1830–1860 was one of reform and humanitarianism.
The Maine Law spurred temperance workers in every state to greater
and ever hopeful activity; the Fugitive Slave Law, the Kansas-
Nebraska Act and the Dred Scott decision fired the opponents of
slavery with zeal; the Women's Rights Convention at Seneca Falls
in 1848 initiated the formal and conscious effort for women's rights.
All these reformers and others, including those for whom education
was "The Cause," recognized the need for education. It was a period,
too, when women were demanding a reconsideration of their status
and of the range of their activities and were seeking a place in public
affairs. It was a period of far reaching educational developments, as
the rise of the common school, the growth of public high schools for
girls as well as boys, the development of normal schools, the establishment of colleges in every section of the country and even of
coeducational colleges and colleges for women. There were educational experiments, inspired both by European and American educa-

tors, and by the belief that education was a great democratizing force. Education was of vital interest to the people of the mid-nineteenth century and the popular periodicals reflected this interest.

Whether these magazines led in any educational reforms, it is difficult to determine. Influence is hard to trace. Nor is space allotment necessarily significant. A clever cartoon is more effective than a verbose article. People are more readily influenced when a new idea is slipped among the familiar ones to which they give habitual acceptance. The best presentation of new ideas may be the casual and incidental. Consequently, any quantitative treatment of the ideas on education in the popular periodicals would not be significant. The important thing is to know what the ideas were.

Therefore, an attempt has been made in this study to give as objectively as possible ideas on education, presented to the laity, especially the ladies. However, as the study is made from the point of view of the reader, it is not completely objective. The ideas have been selected and they have been arranged. The selection has been inclusive, so inclusive that so far as is humanly possible no idea has been omitted. The arrangement, however, is by topics,—the topics currently discussed in the lecture-halls, seminars and workshops of mid-twentieth century teachers colleges and schools of education.

Since few of the magazines have survived, they have been described to provide a setting for the study. Then the basic philosophy of education has been discussed under the topic "What Is Education?" A hundred years ago the vexing matter of woman's "sphere" colored attitudes on female education and curricula for girls. Consequently, the next two chapters deal with the importance of female education and the curricula for young ladies. At a time when public education was in its infancy, education, especially of an experimental nature, flourished only under private auspices. In a sense public education was itself the greatest experiment of all and the public training of teachers was a necessary adjunct thereto. The training of children was of vital interest to parents as well as to teachers. Medical education of women was supported by the women editors and challenged by the men. All—editors and readers—were interested in the education of the handicapped and even the ladies showed interest in exclusively male education. Some of the topics today have only an historic interest; others have a contemporary significance.

It is hoped that this study of ideas on education in magazines for ladies and other popular periodicals may make a humble contribution to American social, intellectual, and educational history.

It remains for me to thank the libraries which have permitted me to read their magazines: American Philosophical Society, Boston Public Library, Carl Schurz Memorial Foundation, Philadelphia, Carnegie Library of Pittsburgh, Columbia University Library, Teachers College Library of Columbia University, Library of Congress, Library of the University of Chicago, Minnesota Historical Society, Moravian Archives, Bethlehem, Library of the State of New York, Newberry Library, Chicago, New York Public Library, New York Society Library, Historical Society of Pennsylvania, Free Library of Philadelphia, Library Company of Philadelphia, Presbyterian Historical Society of Philadelphia, Swarthmore College Library, and the Library of the University of Pennsylvania. To several of these libraries and to the American Antiquarian Society of Worcester, the Massachusetts Historical Society, the Pedagogical Library of Philadelphia, the Library of the Philadelphia High School for Girls, and the Wagner Institute of Philadelphia, I am indebted for other courtesies.

Several librarians have given me aid in excess of that required by courtesy and scholarship. I should like especially to thank Dr. R. W. G. Vail, formerly librarian of the Library of the State of New York and now at the New York Historical Society, Rose Demorest of the Carnegie Library of Pittsburgh, Lois M. Fawcett, Head of the Reference Department of the Minnesota Historical Society, Bess Finn of the Public Service Department of Newberry Library, Chicago, Dr. Kenneth Hamilton of Moravian Archives, the reading room staff of the New York Historical Society and at the Historical Society of Pennsylvania, the reference librarians at Columbia University and at the University of Pennsylvania, and the staff of the magazine room of the Free Library of Philadelphia.

I should also like to thank the department of history of Teachers College, Columbia University, especially Professor Erling M. Hunt under whose direction this study has been made. Throughout its preparation, he has been a constructive critic and stimulating adviser. I am grateful to Professors R. Freeman Butts, Harry J. Carman, Ida A. Jewett, and Carlton C. Qualey of Columbia University for giving the entire study the benefit of careful and critical reading. My friends, too, have been helpful in giving criticism, encouragement, and suggestions.

For errors in citation, interpretation, and judgment, I alone am responsible. After working with magazines for nearly four years, I find that I can give a heart-felt response to the historian's addition to the Litany, as suggested by Frank Luther Mott: "From mistakes of omission and commission, from slips in dates, from transposition of citations, from blunders obvious and recondite, Good Lord, deliver us!"

Contents

CHAPTER ONE

The Magazines and Their Editors [1]

HE MAGAZINE for ladies in the United States—north, south, east, and west—in the decades before the Civil War was *Godey's Lady's Book*.[2] Was it not named *The Lady's Book*, with an accent on "the" and did not the astute Mr. Godey tell his readers that it was "the book of the nation" [3] and keep them informed of its ever growing circulation until in January 1860, he could with joy "wish his hundred and fifty thousand subscribers the compliments of the season"? [4] The understanding Mr. Godey did not for a moment think every lady read her own *Lady's Book*.[5] In January 1859 he estimated the readers at half a million.[6] Not only did he tell them the value of his product,[7] he published complimentary correspondence from readers and from fellow editors,[8] noted that Peterson's Book Store in Philadelphia sold thousands of the *Lady's Book*

1. Not all the magazines used in this study are described in this chapter. An alphabetical list of magazines used is provided in bibliography. See page 140.

2. Bertha Monica Stearns, "Southern Magazines for Ladies (1819–1860)" in *South Atlantic Quarterly,* vol. XXXI, no. 1, January 1932, p. 70.

3. Frank Luther Mott, *A History of American Magazines* (Cambridge, Massachusetts, Harvard University Press, 1939, 3 vols.), vol. I, p. 581.

4. *Godey's Lady's Book,* vol. LX, no. 1, January 1860, p. 85; Isabelle Webb Entriken, *Sarah Josepha Hale and Godey's Lady's Book* (Philadelphia, University of Pennsylvania, doctoral dissertation, 160 pp.), p. 121.

5. *Godey's Lady's Book,* vol. LI, no. 5, November 1855, pp. 425–427, "The Life and Adventures of a Number of Godey's Lady's Book, Addressed particularly to Borrowers, Having been taken down in short-hand from a Narration Made by Itself, when the Unfortunate Creature was in a Cruel and Dilapidated State from Treatment Received at the Hands of Cruel and Oppressed."

6. *Ibid.,* vol. LVIII, no. 1, January 1859, p. 79.

7. *Ibid.,* vol. XX, no. 6, June 1840, p. 284.

8. *Ibid.,* vol. XLIV, no. 4, April 1852, pp. 296–298.

each month,[9] and that copies were sent to Europe and the West Indies.[10] Publishers of other fashion magazines, as *Graham's* and *Peterson's,* paid him the compliment of imitation.[11] At least two aspirants for the approval of the feminine West, *Moore's Western Lady's Book* of Cincinnati and the *Lady's Western Magazine and Garland of the Valley* which in 1848 and 1849 addressed the ladies of Milwaukee and Chicago, were more successful in copying the name of his magazine than the features in which Mr. Godey took such pride. When the editor of a crusading journal wished to boom her circulation, *Godey's* was usually placed first on the list of those magazines with which it was clubbed.[12] The North-Western Union Agricultural Society was the fifth organization to offer it as a premium.[13] Whether or not all feminine America eagerly awaited each issue, as the readers were led to suppose, may be open to question, but there can be no doubt that its leadership was recognized. Nor did it keep its place without reason.

It was a size convenient to handle. Each page was six by nine inches. While the number of pages varied, most issues in the 1850's were about a hundred pages. The modest cover of drab tan or brown, with its conventionalized design or line drawing, gave just a hint of the grandeur that was within—at least one hand-tinted, beautiful fashion plate, several mezzotints of ladies' and gentlemen's fashionable attire, a steel engraving of a famous painting or an interesting place, and at times a beautiful colored print of flowers. These embellishments—the one considered best was the frontispiece; all were at the front of the book—gave to the magazine a distinction worthy of display on the parlor table. They in no way illustrated the text; rather did the text illustrate them. In the finest print, usually near the back, were minute descriptions of the fashions and comments on the painting, artist, or building.

While the fashion magazines were embellished in much the same way, each publisher deemed his product infinitely superior to those

---

9. *Ibid.,* vol. XLVII, no. 2, August 1853, p. 184.
10. *Ibid.,* vol. XLVII, no. 6, December 1853, p. 560.
11. A comparison of the issues of any year makes this apparent.
12. *Sibyl,* vol. II, no. 2, July 15, 1857, p. 206; no. 4, August 15, 1857, p. 224.
13. *Godey's Lady's Book,* vol. LVI, May 1858, p. 470.

of his rivals. In fact Mr. Godey probably looked upon Messrs.
Graham, Peterson, Post, et. al. as mere upstarts. Although many
of the embellishments represent the artistic ideals of a past age,
they might, when placed beside the pictorial features of a modern
magazine, even be preferred.

This is not true of other features of the format. In the days of
hand-set type, a smaller type was used; capital letters were an
eighth of an inch in height, small letters a sixteenth, or to borrow the
nomenclature of the printer, the body type was seven-point Scotch
Roman. [This book is set in Scotch Roman.] Although the "shoul-
der," the mechanical device which produces a white space between
lines, had not yet been invented, the leading between the lines helped
the reader. The fashion magazines were usually printed with small
margins in two columns with about a quarter of an inch between
columns. They are a little more easily read than the modern tele-
phone book. This kind of printing was, of course, common to all the
magazines and newspapers of the time. The size of the paper and
the number of the columns varied. Magazines which were the size
of newspapers, like *The Home Journal,* had nine instead of the
eight columns of today. Although the rag paper has valiantly with-
stood the ravages of time, the pages, yellow with age, increase the
difficulties of the modern reader. Yet the print alone suggests that
the phrase, "poring over one's book," may not necessarily have had
its origin in complete absorption in the matter.

The style, however, of many of the writers did demand close attention. Mrs. Sarah Josepha Hale, who wielded her editorial pen
from 1828, when she became editor of her *Lady's Magazine,* until
1871, when she retired as editor of *Godey's Lady's Book,* set the
fashion for writers in ladies' magazines. She was a master of the art
of circumlocution and many of her sentences were grammatical
achievements. Nothing that she wrote, however, had the opaque
quality of the output of some of her editorial brethren.

It is not without significance that in 1837, the year Queen Victoria
ascended the throne, Mrs. Hale, queen of editresses, should have
ascended to the editorial chair of what many considered the queen
of ladies' magazines. The two women, born as they were to very dif-

ferent stations in life, as Mrs. Hale would have put it, were not unlike. There is probably no one whose writings more nearly typify the ideas generally associated with the queen than those of Sarah Josepha Hale. She shared the editorship with Louis A. Godey throughout her association with the *Lady's Book,* she as literary editor, he as publisher and general manager.[14] Others, like Morton McMichael and Mrs. Lydia H. Sigourney, had only a passing editorial association.

Nothing was admitted to the *Lady's Book* that was not "pure." With what satisfaction must the editor in 1860 have quoted a letter indicative of her success in which the writer said, "You have succeeded in raising the character of *a* Lady's Book from a mere collection of pleasant stories, for whiling away the hours, to a monthly director of the taste and morals and a heightened standard of what is truly womanly. . . ." [15] This "truly womanly" character was apparent on every page of the *Lady's Book* from the "embellishments" and music through the "literature"—fiction, poetry, biographical sketches, etc.—to the diagrams for making clothes, the instructions for fancy work, "receipts," which gave no specific directions, news of Philadelphia fashions, and the intimate chit-chat with the editors. In these columns Mrs. Hale, and at times Mr. Godey as publisher, expressed views on many subjects, especially those of a nonsectional sensitivity. It was probably this policy which gave the *Lady's Book* preeminence in the South even on the eve of the Civil War, a preeminence deplored by Southern writers.[16]

While Godey's "contemporaries"—*Graham's, Miss Leslie's, Peterson's* and *Arthur's* in Philadelphia, *The Ladies' Companion, Sargent's New Monthly Magazine of Literature, Fashion and Fine Arts,* and *Columbian Lady's and Gentleman's Magazine* in New York, and *Sartain's Union Magazine,* published first in New York then in Philadelphia—were slavish imitators, they did not use scissors and paste for pen and pencil, as most of the other ladies' maga-

14. Mott, *op. cit.,* vol. I, p. 584.
15. *Godey's Lady's Book,* vol. LXI, no. 6, December 1860, p. 555.
16. *DeBow's Review and Industrial Resources, Statistics, etc.,* vol. XXIX o.s., vol. IV n.s., no. 2, August 1860, p. 221.

zines had done for years. *Graham's* and the *Columbian* catered to
men as well as women and were largely directed by men. Their
fashion plates were as beautiful but descriptions were sometimes
lacking and rarely were so detailed. The Editors' Table wasn't the
same; they had no Mrs. Hale. Graham began the policy in 1841 of
presenting original steel engravings, in contrast to those which had
been used.[17] He paid his contributors liberally and thus secured
some of the best writers of the time. Poe, while literary editor in
the 1840's did some of his best work for *Graham's*. *Peterson's*, a two
dollar magazine, founded in 1842, and *Arthur's*, established ten
years later, did not at first offer the same competition to *Godey's* as
did *Graham's*. After the Civil War, however, *Peterson's*, whose
fashion plates were quite as attractive as *Godey's*, and whose editor
and publisher had learned the art of pleasing the ladies from
Mr. Godey, outstripped its three dollar rival.[18]

Although Poe, Longfellow, Lowell and Whittier contributed at
times to these magazines, there was a remarkable sameness about
most of the "literature," written by such lesser lights as T. S. Arthur, Elizabeth Oaks Smith, Eliza Leslie and Joseph C. Neal.
Nearly all the stories dealt with "LOVE"; all were success stories;
all had a happy ending. To the writers and readers of the ladies'
magazines, success meant just one thing,—marriage and living
happily ever afterward. There were, of course, exceptions. The
self-sacrificing heroine might forego marriage in order to care for an
invalid parent or orphaned younger brothers or sisters. The wife
might endure a drunken husband; the daughter, a drunken father.
These women, too, had their rewards. If the mother did not die or
the father was not killed in time for the heroine to marry the town's
most eligible bachelor or rich widower, the author left no doubt in
the mind of the reader that she would receive her reward in the next
world. A woman could attain happiness either in this world or the
next only in relation to others, and the crucial person was always a
man—husband, father, son. The same emphasis was present in the
biographical accounts of women of the Revolution and the frontier

17. Mott, *op. cit.*, vol. I, p. 547.
18. *Ibid.*, vol. II, p. 309.

which Mrs. Ellet and others wrote for the ladies' magazines.[19] Most
of the verse—its only claim to poetry lay in the rhyming of the lines
—proclaimed the same sentiment. When the ideas and ideals that
were placed before the women and girls are considered, the wonder
is that there were any rumblings in the direction of self-expression.

But efforts were made to shape a new pattern. Sarah Josepha
Hale was a pioneer. When the death of her husband left her with
five children to support, she became a partner in a millinery shop
and a contributor to annuals and magazines.[20] In 1828 she began to
edit her *Ladies' Magazine*. One of her aims was to educate women.
Not only did she campaign for education, especially that of girls,
but she constantly endeavored to educate her readers by keeping
them informed of the movements and activities of the time,[21] and
by directing their tastes. Even fashion plates were used to indicate
good taste.[22]

Mrs. Hale was not the first editress in America to launch a periodical addressed to her own sex. In November 1814, Mrs. Mary
Clarke Carr, a Philadelphian, presented *The Intellectual Regale or
Ladies' Tea Tray*, a weekly magazine to two hundred subscribers.
Largely through her own efforts she kept the *Intellectual Regale*
alive for a year. She offered essays, anecdotes, sketches and verse
and was careful to mark her own contributions with an "o" for
"original." She began the custom of chatting intimately with her
readers and even condemned the ladies of Philadelphia for their
lack of literary taste and indicated that the women of New York
were far more discerning in that they supported three literary
miscellanies.[23] Yet editresses seemed to try their wings in other

19. *Godey's Lady's Book*, vol. XXXVI, no. 1, January 1848, pp. 11–19;
no. 2, February 1848, pp. 77–79; no. 3, March 1848, pp. 145–148; no. 4, April
1848, pp. 240–242; no. 5, May 1848, pp. 300–302; no. 6, June 1848, pp. 321–
323; vol. XXXVII, no. 1, July 1848, pp. 6–9; no. 2, August 1848, pp. 69–70;
no. 3, September 1848, pp. 167–168; vol. XLIV, no. 4, October 1852, pp.
370–375; vol. LIV, no. 4, April 1857, pp. 339–341, etc.

20. Entriken, *op. cit.*, pp. 9 ff.

21. *The Ladies' Magazine*, vol. I, no. 1, January 1828, pp. 3 ff.

22. Lawrence Martin, "The Genesis of Godey's Lady's Book" in *The New
England Quarterly Review*, vol. I, no. 1, January 1928, pp. 41–79 (citation
p. 54), and *Ladies' Magazine*, vol. III, no. 11, November 1830, frontispiece.

23. Bertha Monica Stearns, "Early Philadelphia Magazines for Ladies" in

cities than New York. In 1830–1831, Mrs. Mary Chase Burney of Baltimore edited *The National Magazine or Ladies' Emporium* and invited Marylanders of both sexes to lend generous aid in contributing to the literary department or in giving a well-written review.[24] Thus by the year 1830, the year that *Godey's* was established,[25] two important characteristics of magazines for ladies had been introduced by women editors, the intimate relationship between editor and readers, called by various names—Editor's Table, Chit-Chat—and the welcoming of contributions from men as well as women. While Mrs. Hale tried to encourage women writers, men made frequent contributions to the *Lady's Book*. Mrs. Jane Swisshelm awarded a prize of one hundred dollars [26] to Dr. John K. Townsend of Philadelphia for his "Tale of Waskamah or the Red Rose of the Shoshones" which began in *The Pittsburgh Saturday Visiter* on Saturday, October 20, 1849 and delighted the readers for several months.[27] Men seem to have been welcome as unpaid contributors in all women's magazines.

This relationship of *Godey's* and other ladies' magazines to these early magazines for ladies is important to note, for at least one twentieth-century critic sees them as the outgrowth of the annual or gift book.[28] That they owe a debt to the humbler magazines for ladies,[29] as well as to the elaborate annuals with their gilded edges, floral prints, and steel engravings, can scarcely be doubted. Both magazines for ladies and annuals copied copiously even from them-

---

The Pennsylvania Magazine of History and Biography, vol. LXIV, no. 4, October 1940, pp. 484–486.

24. *The National Magazine or Ladies' Emporium,* vol. I, no. 1, November 1830, p. 3.

25. Mott, *op. cit.,* vol. I, p. 800; *Godey's Lady's Book,* vol. I, no. 1, July 1830.

26. *Pittsburgh Saturday Visiter,* vol. II, no. 30, August 11, 1849, p. 117.

27. *Ibid.,* vol. II, no. 35, September 15, 1849, p. 138; no. 36, September 22, 1849, p. 142; no. 40, October 20, 1849, p. 160 and subsequent issues.

28. Fred Lewis Pattee, *The Feminine Fifties* (New York, D. Appleton–Century Company, 1940, pp. x, 339), p. 276; Fred Lewis Pattee, *The First Century of American Literature, 1770–1870* (New York, D. Appleton–Century Company, 1935, pp. viii, 613), pp. 391–392.

29. Bertha Monica Stearns, "Early Philadelphia Magazines for Ladies" in *The Pennsylvania Magazine of History and Biography,* vol. LXIV, no. 4, October 1940, p. 491.

selves. In 1841 Henry W. Herbert of New York committed *The Magnolia* "to that atmosphere which may doom it to be blighted by the frost of the first winter; but which *will*, it is hoped, permit it to bloom again, and with a beauty more mature, than it presumes to boast in this its infant blossoming." [30] It "bloomed" in exactly the same form, except for change of date, in 1842, 1843, 1844. This repetition may not have mattered, for the pressed flowers and uncut pages that the modern reader comes upon are not without significance.

Floral names were given to magazines as well as to annuals. *The Southern Rose Bud*,[31] "devoted to the culture of the imagination, the understanding and the heart," was begun by Mrs. Caroline Gillman in Charleston, South Carolina in September 1832. It "enlarged and matured" to *The Southern Rose* [32] in 1835, but withered and died in 1839, because its editor preferred "some mode of publication less exacting than the rigorous punctuality of periodical work." [33] It was a leaflet in form; originally it was eight pages, issued every Saturday; but beginning with volume III in order to "admit pieces of greater length and save half the postage" it was issued on a double sheet every two weeks.[34] The size of each page varied: $10\frac{1}{4}$ inches by 6 inches, volume II, no. 1, August 31, 1833; 8 inches by $5\frac{1}{4}$ inches, volume 7, number 1, September 1, 1838; $9\frac{1}{2}$ inches by 6 inches, volume 7, no. 23, July 6, 1839. No matter what its size the cost of subscription was two dollars and a half a year.

Several of the ladies' magazines varied in size, name and periodicity. Most of the editors of these smaller magazines performed their labors in conjunction with their daily tasks. An issue might be late because of the birth or illness of a child, but since the editor explained the situation quite frankly to her readers, they appear

30. *The Magnolia,* edited by Henry W. Herbert (New York, Published by A. and C. B. Edwards, No. 3 Park Row, Aaron Guest, Printer) advertisement facing cover of book issued in 1841.

31. *The Southern Rose Bud,* vol. II, no. 1, August 31, 1833, p. 1.

32. *Ibid.,* vol. III, no. 26, August 22, 1835, p. 206.

33. *Southern Rose,* vol. 7, no. 26, August 17, 1839, p. 416.

34. *Southern Rose Bud,* vol. II, no. 48, July 26, 1834, p. 191.

from their letters to have shared the joy or sorrow, rather than to have been censorious.[35] A few magazines seem to have been published whenever there was material. *The Ladies' Miscellany,* published for the ladies of Salem, Massachusetts, for a dollar a year, supposedly was a four page weekly, yet the first number of volume one was issued Friday, November 7, 1828; the second, beginning remarkably with page 7, Tuesday, January 6, 1829, while the fifty-second number of volume two came out on March 30, 1831. Except for the professionally edited magazines, the unexpected in date of issue, paging, and the numbering of volumes with Roman numerals or Arabic was sufficiently frequent to remove any element of surprise. The contents were far less novel, so successful were the scissors and the "pruning knife!" [36]

Midway between the fashion magazines on the one hand and the hopeful efforts of the frequently self-appointed editors on the other, was *The Ladies' Garland,* "a wreath of many flowers devoted to literature, amusement, and instruction," [37] published in Philadelphia from 1837 to 1849 for a dollar a year. Its contents were largely "selected," although Mrs. Lydia Jane Pierson, Mrs. Lydia H. Sigourney,[38] and T. S. Arthur [39] contributed. It was far inferior to *Godey's, Graham's,* and *Peterson's* and varied in form from a newspaper to an annual and in periodicity from ten irregular issues in 1837, to semi-annual (1846–1849) and annual volumes (1838 and 1843).

Another kind of ladies' magazine was that edited by clergymen. *The Ladies' Pearl,* which the Reverend Daniel Wise edited in Lowell, Massachusetts, from 1840 to 1842, was an individual venture which closed its first volume with a subscription list of four

35. *Pittsburgh Saturday Visiter,* vol. II, no. 39, October 12, 1849, p. 154 (charming editorial about her three-day-old baby by the editor, Mrs. Swisshelm); no. 41, October 27, 1849, p. 154 (note of apology—baby had been ill).

36. A department of the *Southern Rose.*

37. *The Ladies' Garland,* vol. I, no. 1, April 15, 1837, p. 1.

38. Mott, *op. cit.,* vol. I, p. 672.

39. *The Ladies' Garland,* vol. II, no. 1, July 1844, pp. 13–15, and no. 2, August 1844, pp. 33–35, "The Wine Party" by T. S. Arthur. Written for *Ladies' Garland.*

thousand.[40] It was "devoted to the pleasure and profit of WOMAN" but did not "refuse to take an occasional jaunt into the fairy land of fiction." [41] It provided the Reverend Mr. Wise with a suitable resting place for his sermons.

In fact furnishing a repository for sermons gave a similarity to all clerically edited magazines. The editor of *The Presbyterian Casket of Sacred and Polite Literature,* the Reverend S. A. Hodgman of St. Louis, Missouri, considered the "sermons alone in The Casket worth the price of the money," one dollar a year. At the end of the first year, he expressed satisfaction in the accomplishment of the "original design, to afford a substitute for the light and trashy literature so eagerly sought for and so dearly paid for in the embellished and glittering magazines of the day." [42] It is interesting to note that in two parts of the country, the West [43] and the South,[44] except for *Godey's,* the most popular ladies' magazines were edited by Methodist clergymen. The *Ladies' Repository* was founded in 1841 at Cincinnati [45] and the *Southern Lady's Companion* was edited from 1847 to 1854 by the Reverend H. M. Henkle for the Methodist Church South at Nashville, Tennessee.[46] Both encouraged contributions from readers. They provided numerous erudite but not ponderous articles, poems, book reviews, an occasional wood-cut by way of illustration, and a selection of music. They preserved commencement addresses as well as sermons. *The Ladies' Repository* shunned fiction but the *Southern Lady's Companion* admitted a few well-chosen stories. *The Universalist and Ladies' Repository,* published under the auspices of the Universalist Church in Boston, was in the 1840's and 1850's as much like the *Ladies'*

40. *Ladies' Pearl,* vol. II, no. 1, July 1841, p. 23.

41. *Ibid.,* vol. II, no. 9, March 1842, pp. 214–215.

42. *The Presbyterian Casket of Sacred and Polite Literature,* vol. II, no. VI, March 1851, back of cover.

43. Bertha Monica Stearns, "Early Western Magazines for Ladies" in the *Mississippi Valley Historical Review,* vol. XVIII, no. 3, December 1931, p. 328.

44. Bertha Monica Stearns, "Southern Magazines for Ladies, 1819–1860" in *The South Atlantic Quarterly,* vol. XXXI, no. 1, January 1932, pp. 82–83.

45. Mott, *op. cit.,* vol. II, p. 301.

46. File of *Southern Lady's Companion.*

Repository as its name would imply. All of these magazines had as their aim the development of a well-rounded Christian womanhood.

In sharp contrast to the clerically edited magazines were the publications that aimed at moral reform. *The Friend of Virtue,* a semi-monthly, was edited in the 1840's by Miss Rebecca Eaton, corresponding secretary of the New England Moral Reform Society and carried as a sub-heading the first verse of the 119th Psalm, "Blessed are the undefiled in the way that walk in the law of the Lord." *The Advocate of Moral Reform* was published in New York by the American Female Moral Reform Society, and had as its motto, "Blessed are the pure in heart for they shall see God" (Matthew V: 8). The subscription to each was a dollar a year; both were eight pages in length. To the ladies of the Moral Reform Society, whether in Boston or in New York, moral reform meant obedience to the seventh commandment; both fixed the responsibility for such obedience upon woman. The events of the day, the "disgraceful frontispiece" of *Godey's Lady's Book,*[47] the unfortunate mode of life in the Sandwich Islands,[48] and the innumerable accounts of the girl "who had made one false step" were viewed from only one angle. One can but wonder whether their very concentration may not have defeated their aims. About the time of the Civil War the editors of both magazines ceased to pursue the erring and dwelt on the delights of the home. *The Friend of Virtue* became *The Home Guardian.*

Equally in earnest but in a positive rather than a negative way were the women editors who labored in the cause of women's rights. These crusaders usually championed other causes first. Mrs. Jane Grey Swisshelm, editor of the *Pittsburgh Saturday Visiter* from 1849 until 1852, battled valiantly against slavery and only secondarily for women's rights. She and Mrs. Amelia Jenks Bloomer, who, during the same period, edited *The Lily* at Seneca Falls, New York, were friendly critics. They challenged each other's ideas, yet encouraged each other. To Mrs. Bloomer the great evil of the day was intemperance, not slavery. Both women wrote from observation.

47. *Advocate of Moral Reform,* vol. VII, no. 16, August 15, 1841, p. 122.
48. *Ibid.,* vol. VII, no. 5, whole no. 137, March 1, 1841, p. 33.

During a two year residence in Louisville, Kentucky, Mrs. Swiss-helm had learned to hate slavery.[49] The evils of intemperance must have been most apparent in Seneca Falls. Mrs. Bloomer and Mrs. Swisshelm were logical in their attacks, but their methods were different. Mrs. Swisshelm appealed to the jury of popular opinion and used many of the tricks of a clever lawyer. Her technique seems to have been to hit hard, and when challenged—to hit harder. There was nothing boring about her spicy paper. "Strength, clearness, aptness, with the elevation and glow of a high pitched purpose, and an impassioned spirit characterized her style." [50] Mrs. Bloomer admired her "dare-devil independence." [51] Mrs. Swisshelm stated that one of her cardinal sins was "exposing Webster as a drunkard and a libertine." [52] Yet she could be tender, as in the advice she gave to country girls,[53] or in encouraging Mrs. Bloomer. "Don't you do it! Mrs. Bloomer! If you do, you will rue it—mind!—Give up *Lily*—because you are subject to headaches." Thus she began a pleasant, complimentary editorial on *The Lily* and concluded by recommending a long subscription list or black coffee.[54] Mrs. Bloomer like Mrs. Swisshelm had a keen sense of humor but her wit was not so caustic. Her good nature helped her to keep her sense of proportion. She cleverly parried the editorial jests brought forth by her espousal of the Bloomer costume. This championship boomed the circulation of *The Lily* to four thousand but brought

49. Arthur J. Larsen, editor, *Crusader and Feminist, Letters of Jane Grey Swisshelm, 1858–1865* (Saint Paul, Minnesota Historical Society, 1934, 327 pp.) p. 3.
50. Quoted from *National Era* in *Pittsburgh Saturday Visiter*, vol. II, no. 2, January 27, 1849, p. 6.
51. Elizabeth Cady Stanton, Susan B. Anthony, Matilda Joslyn Gage, *History of Woman Suffrage* (Rochester, Fowler and Wells, 1881, 4 volumes) vol. I, pp. 844–845.
52. *Pittsburgh Saturday Visiter*, vol. IV, no. XXXIX, October 18, 1851, p. 154. A two columned editorial appeared in vol. III, no. 19, May 25, 1850, p. 74.
53. "Letters to Country Girls" in *Pittsburgh Saturday Visiter*, vol. II, no. 8, March 10, 1849, p. 30; no. 10, March 24, 1849, p. 38; no. 11, March 31, 1849, p. 42; no. 12, April 7, 1849, p. 46; no. 13, April 14, 1849, p. 50; no. 14, April 21, 1849, p. 58, etc.
54. *Ibid.*, vol. III, no. 35, September 14, 1850, p. 138.

adverse criticism and ridicule.[55] When the attacks on her reform
dress took attention away from more important matters, Mrs.
Bloomer returned to customary feminine attire.[56] After she left
Seneca Falls, she continued to edit *The Lily* at Mt. Vernon, Ohio,
until 1854, when she was succeeded by Mrs. Mary Birdsall of
Richmond, Indiana, who kept *The Lily* alive until 1856.

Another contemporary of *The Lily* was *The Una*. Between 1853
and 1856, under the editorship of Mrs. Paulina Wright Davis of
Providence, Rhode Island, and her assistant and successor, Mrs.
Caroline Dall of Boston, it proclaimed its interest in the "elevation
of woman." *The Una* was named for the heroine of the first book of
Spenser's *Fairy Queen,* who impersonated truth in "that exquisite
allegory." [57] Mrs. Davis, as befitted one interested in the elevation
of woman, was logical, clear and learned. Her articles sound not
unlike the brief of a lawyer who has prepared his case to be argued
before a learned judge. She frequently used deductive reasoning,
in contrast to the inductive approach of Mrs. Bloomer and Mrs.
Swisshelm. Mrs. Swisshelm thought *The Una* a little heavy, for
said she, "People do not want a whole meal of one dish, or a whole
paper on one subject." [58] When *The Lily* purchased the subscription list of *The Una,* the editor commented: "The two papers have
been essentially different in their characteristics, though working
for the same great principles of Truth and Justice. While *The Lily*
with earnest simplicity, has dealt mainly with the practical interests
of Woman . . . The Una has dealt more with principles and policy
from which grew her wrongs and in high toned scholastic essays
shown the grand tone of her rights. We would combine, somewhat,
the two characters and thereby offer a paper suited to the tastes
and wants of a still wider circle of readers . . ." [59]

A fourth crusading periodical was *The Sibyl,* the official organ
of the National Dress Reform League.[60] Although in the first issue,

55. Dexter C. Bloomer, *Life and Writings of Amelia Bloomer* (Boston,
Arena Publishing Co., 1895, 387 pp.) pp. 84 ff.
56. *Ibid.,* p. 70.   57. *The Una,* vol. II, no. 2, February 1854, pp. 112–113.
58. Quoted in *The Una,* vol. III, no. 2, February 1854, p. 25.
59. *The Lily,* vol. VIII, no. 8, April 15, 1856, p. 2.
60. Mott, *op. cit.,* vol. II, p. 52.

it proclaimed its interest in any reform and it gave support to temperance, anti-slavery, women's rights, education, and hydropathy, its devotion to what it deemed *the* vital reform was apparent in every isue. It was edited at Middletown, New York, from 1856 to 1864 by Drs. Lydia Sayer—the Drs. stood for doctress—who, after her marriage to her printer, added Hasbrouck to her name.

All four of these magazines were like newspapers. The *Saturday Visiter* and the fifth volume of *The Lily* were of newspaper size, and four pages in length. Each page of the others was about half the size but there were about twice as many pages. The subscription price of *The Lily* was fifty cents a year; of the others, a dollar. At the close of the first year the accounts of *The Lily* showed a balance of twenty-four dollars to pay Mrs. Bloomer for a year's worry and work, which included even that of preparing the copies for mailing. While the first volume of *The Lily* contained the caption "published by a committee of ladies," Mrs. Bloomer subsequently stated that before the material for the first issue was gathered, the Ladies' Temperance Society of Seneca Falls had abandoned it to its editor. In order to fulfill the pledge to subscribers, she determined to publish it. About two hundred copies of the first issue were printed. Because of the success of *The Lily* the first year, she decided to continue the paper.[61] Although *The Sibyl* came to be the official organ of the National Dress Reform League, it was begun by Drs. Sayer without a single subscription. She wrote to prominent reformers, suggesting that they aid her, but she subsequently stated, in writing a history of *The Sibyl*: "We are under the painful necessity of saying that not one of these responded to our call at the time, though some months after Mrs. Bloomer wrote us a letter, with

61. In Mrs. Bloomer's copy of *The Lily*, volumes I to IV inclusive, is a clipping from the Chicago *Interocean*, of the "Woman's Kingdom," conducted by Mrs. Elizabeth Boynton Herbert, which was devoted to a letter from Mrs. Amelia Bloomer of Council Bluffs, Iowa, March 4 (the year 1893 can be inferred from other evidence) in which she gave the history of *The Lily*. A manuscript letter to Lillian G. Browne from Mrs. Bloomer, dated Council Bluffs, March 21, 1893 and also at the New York State Library, Albany, gives much the same information. Many of the facts are found in D. C. Bloomer, *Life and Writings of Amelia Bloomer* (Boston, Arena Publishing Company, 1895, p. 387).

apologies on account of ill-health for not responding sooner. A portion of her communication, though intended for the public eye, we did not deem sufficiently interesting, or of the right nature to please or instruct our readers." [62]

The editors of these four crusading journals gave their labor; they literally breathed life into their magazines. There were contributors who, for the most part, were anonymous. At times, they used pen names or signed initials. In November 1849, "Sunflower" began her dialogues between Henry Neil and his mother in *The Lily*,[63] unfolded to "E. C. S." in August 1850,[64] and in July 1851 Mrs. Bloomer announced that "E. C. S." stood for "Elizabeth Cady Stanton." [65]

Anonymity and pen names were the custom of the times rather than a cloak to feminine reticence. "Ada Clare" had a regular column in the *New York Saturday Press;* the sister of N. P. Willis wrote her *Fern Leaves* under the name of "Fanny Fern"; and *Harper's* and the *Atlantic* did not print the names of authors until 1860 and 1862 respectively.[66]

The Atlantic Monthly, begun in 1857, has for nearly a century kept a literary tone and unostentatious appearance. *Harper's New Monthly Magazine* was, from its beginning in June 1850, a leading journal of literature and events. In the 1850's it catered to the ladies by secreting fashion plates near the back, often following "Leaves from Punch" where the same costumes were treated less seriously. Humor was important, too, in *The Knickerbocker Magazine,* which under the editorship of Lewis Gaylord Clark (1834–1860) graciously "usher[ed] others into the presence of the public." [67] Bulwer considered it the best American periodical; Dickens found its pages entertaining.[68] In San Francisco F. C. Ewer hoped

62. *The Sibyl,* vol. I, no. 23, June 1, 1857, p. 180.
63. *The Lily,* vol. I, no. 11, November 1849, p. 86.
64. *Ibid.,* vol. II, no. 8, August 1850, p. 60.
65. *Ibid.,* vol. III, no. 7, July 1851, p. 54.
66. Mott, *op. cit.,* vol. II, p. 26.
67. *The Knickerbocker,* vol. I, no. 1, January 1833, p. 7.
68. *The Western Literary Messenger, a Family Magazine of Literature, Science, Art, Morality and General Intelligence,* vol. XI, no. 1, September 1848, p. 46.

to conduct his *Pioneer Magazine* "as nearly as possible after the style of Knickerbocker," but to use California talent.[69] In 1844 Littell, editor of *The Living Age,* began diligently to clip the best from British reviews for the benefit of the American public. The erudite *North American Review* and the two leading Southern reviews, *Southern Literary Messenger,* of which Poe was editor from December 1835 to January 1837, and *The Southern Quarterly Review,* presented comments on men, events, and letters. *DeBow's Review,* published in New Orleans, was primarily interested in promoting the commercial interests of the South and West but included articles on other subjects and a little "literature." While politics were prominent in *The United States and Democratic Review* and *The American Whig Review,* much that was not political was presented to their readers. Weekly magazines, newspapers in form, as *Frank Leslie's Illustrated Newspaper,* N. P. Willis' *Home Journal,* and the *New York Saturday Press* were welcomed to many homes.

In addition there were several organs of special groups which some of the ladies may have read. *The Free Enquirer* was supported by the few who could stomach the originality of its views. The learned literature of Margaret Fuller's *Dial* appealed to the transcendentalist group. 'The *National Anti-Slavery Standard,* edited during the 1840's by Lydia Maria Child and her husband, David Child, brought its message to opponents of slavery, and the *Pennsylvania Prison Journal* kept its readers informed about efforts to improve the fate of those social outcasts.

Nor were Americans who read French or German allowed to remain in ignorance of the events of the day. Not only had they access to European reviews, but magazines in both languages were published in the United States. In the 1830's two reviews in French were published in New York City, *La Revue Française* and *La France Littéraire. La Revue Française* stated that it would present selections of the whole periodical literature of Europe, presented in

69. *The Pioneer or California Monthly,* vol. I, no. 3, March 1854, no. 4, April 1854, vol. II, no. 5, November 1854, etc. (Advertisement on first page of each issue.)

the French language.[70] From November 1835 to June 1836, it was published by Hoskins and Snowden; but in July 1836, they disposed of their interests to Joseph Alexander Debonnet. *La France Littéraire* was issued by the Bureau de la France from 1835 to 1836. Like *La Review Française,* it brought France and the literature and events of French speaking countries to America. There were occasional articles about events in the United States, but even these came by way of Europe. "Les États-Unis et le President Jackson en 1834" was quoted from the *Foreign Review.*[71] Alexis de Tocqueville in "De la Democratie en Amérique" discussed such topics as the United States government and the suffrage in New England, Louisiana and Georgia.[72] Gustave de Beaumant in "Les Femmes aux États-Unis" compared American women with French, contrasted the freedom of American girls with the sheltered care given to French girls and described briefly the education of American girls which differed entirely from that of the French.[73] The writer left no doubt as to which he considered superior. Both these reviews, even when dealing with the American scene, were more French than American.

The magazines published in German were for German speaking Americans and show their interests. They are both American and German, American in that they reflect the American scene, often with an American attitude, and German in that they are written in German, frequently from a German point of view. Two years after establishing his *Illustrated Newspaper,* Frank Leslie began his *Illustrirte Zeitung,* which he stated was for the German circle of New York. *Illustrirte Zeitung* was not a translation of the English magazine. In 1857, it was edited by Dr. Brandeis, was twelve pages in length and cost five cents in contrast to the sixteen pages and cost of six cents of the *Illustrated Newspaper.* When the two newspapers for the same date are compared, differences are apparent

70. *La Revue Française,* vol. I, no. 1, Novembre 1833, p. 1 (advertisement in English and in French).

71. *La France Littéraire,* Tome Quatrième, Seconde Année (1835) pp. 233–257.

72. *Ibid.,* Tome Sixième, Seconde Année (1835) pp. 241–269.

73. *La Revue Française,* vol. 3, no. 5, Mars 1835, pp. 358–363.

in topics of discussion and presentation. In the issues of September 12, 1857, the Seventh Annual Festival of the Turners at Yorkville Park, begun on August 29 and concluded on September 2, was featured.[74] The same illustrations were used, but the German captions either quoted a proverb or pointed a moral. The picture of men crowding at a window, marked "Tickets for Bier" had these two headings: "Selling Tickets for Lager Beer" and "Die Ersten werden die Letzen und die Letzen die Ersten." A picture of a man, woman and child with beer mugs was "A Family Scene at the picnic" and "Braun Bier gerathen." "A Horn of Lager Bier and a Mug of Lager Bier" became "Donnerwetter, das läuft wie Oel hinunter"; "Kissing Ring at the Picnic" became "Küssen beim Ringspiel, Einen Kuss in Ehren, Kann Niemand verwehren." *Illustrirte Zeitung* had a rival in *Belletristiches Journal, Eine Wochenschrift für Literature, Kunst, Wissenschaft, Politik und Tagegeschichte,* published in New York from 1852 to 1909.

The German publications in the United States show a people who had put forth roots in a new soil. Occasionally, as in *Die Biene,* there was English usage in German, as the use of the apostrophe to denote possession.[75] The two publications of the Moravians in German, *Die Biene* and *Das Brüder-Blatt,* like *The Moravian Church Miscellany,* told of Moravian activities in Pennsylvania and North Carolina and their missionary enterprises throughout the world and gave items of world and local news. Both were edited by Moravian clergy—*Die Biene, Ein Volks-Blatt,* a bi-monthly by the "Reverend Doctor" A. L. Heubner of Bethlehem, and *Das Brüder-Blatt,* a monthly by the Reverend Lavin T. Reichel of Lititz, Pennsylvania and later "Salem, Nord Carolina," and subsequently by Carl F. Seidel in Bethlehem. Although the editor and his residence changed, *Das Brüder-Blatt* was published in Lancaster from 1854 to 1861. *Die Biene* was published in Bethlehem between 1846 and 1848.

Another publication in German, *Blätter für Freies Religiöses*

---

74. *Frank Leslie's Illustrated Newspaper,* vol. IV, no. 95, September 12, 1857, pp. 228–239; *Frank Leslie's Illustrirte Zeitung,* Band 1, no. 4, 12 September 1857, pp. 37–43.

75. *Die Biene,* Band I, no. 10, den. 9 mai 1846, p. 78.

Leben was the work of Friedrich Schünemann-Pott of Philadelphia on the eve of the Civil War. More than twenty years earlier, two German magazines were published in Baltimore, *Der Amerikanisch-Deutsch Hausfreund und Baltimore Calendar* and *Dideskalia*. *Der Hausfreund* (1835–1844) was more like an almanac than a magazine. *Dideskalia* was published "für Geist, Gemüth and Publicität der Deutschen in den Vereinigten-Staaten." One of the most informative of the German magazines, however, was *Atlantis,* "Eine Monatschrift für Wissenschaft, Politik und Poesie," published in Buffalo from 1854 to 1858. *Illustrirte Abend-Schule,* an eight-page magazine, usually a bimonthly, was also published in Buffalo from 1854 to 1857, when it was moved to St. Louis. It might seem from the title as if *Die Abend-Schule* were intended for children, but L. Lange who published it in St. Louis and his predecessor in Buffalo had a broad conception of "Schule" and stated that it was "eine Zeitschrift für Belehrung und Unterhaltung." Through much of 1855 a serialized account of Christopher Columbus [76] was featured, while briefer mention was made of the work of Elihu Burritt,[77] Alexander II of Russia,[78] and Frémont.[79] Items of geography, history, current history, art, architecture and biology were given in *Die Abend-Schule.*

Of the magazines devoted to education, *The American Annals of Education and Instruction,* edited from 1832 to 1837 by William C. Woodbridge, the *Common School Journal,* edited by Horace Mann, and the journals edited at times by Henry Barnard—*The Connecticut Common School Journal, Journal of Rhode Island Institute of Instruction,* and *American Journal of Education*—were the most quoted by lay and professional periodicals alike. In fact, Mann, Henry Barnard, and F. A. P. Barnard, who before the Civil War was at the University of Alabama, were considered the authorities on education.

76. *Illustrirte Abend-Schule,* Jahrgang 2, no. 1, den 17ten Februar 1855, p. 1; no. 2, den 10ten Marz 1855, p. 9, etc.

77. *Ibid.,* no. 3, den 17ten Marz, 1855, p. 21.

78. *Ibid.,* no. 5, 14ten April 1855, p. 36 (article), p. 37 (picture).

79. *Ibid.,* no. 6, den 28ten April 1855, pp. 43–44.

These were, of course, not all the periodicals of the period, but they represented every type of magazine and every section of the country. Philadelphia was the acknowledged center of the fashion magazines and the average annual circulation of her journals exceeded those of other cities.[80] Boston with such magazines as *The North American Review, The Dial, Littell's Living Age,* and *The Atlantic* considered herself a leader of thought, but by the eve of the Civil War, New York with *Knickerbocker's, Harper's* and *The Home Journal* had begun to challenge her position. Baltimore, Richmond, Charleston, New Orleans, and Cincinnati were important centers.

In the pre-Civil War days, when the territory between the Appalachians and the Mississippi was "the West," a West which was youthfully and painfully conscious of the literary leadership of the East, there were many attempts at magazine literature. Cincinnati, which "assumed to be the literary Queen of the West," [81] mothered the more successful journals, as Timothy Flint's *Western Monthly Magazine, The Western Monthly Magazine, a Continuation of the Illinois Monthly Magazine,* which was resuscitated in Cincinnati in 1830, survived until 1837, when it died after removal to Louisville, the *Western Literary Journal,* edited by William D. Gallagher in 1836, and two of the most successful western ladies' magazines, *Moore's Lady's Magazine* and the *Ladies' Repository. The Western Messenger,* published first at Cincinnati and then at Louisville was the most important magazine of the West between 1835 and 1841 [82] as well as an official organ of the Unitarian Church. Jesse Clement's *Western Literary Messenger* of Buffalo excelled in length of life many of Cincinnati's publications (1841–1857). Detroit with Wellman's *Literary Miscellany* (1849–1854) and Mrs. Electra M. Sheldon's *Western Literary Cabinet* (1853–1854) and St. Louis with *The Western Casket* (December 1850—through 1854) and *The Western Journal of Agriculture, Manufacture, Mechanic Arts, Internal Improvement, Commerce, and General Literature* challenged

---

80. Mott, *op. cit.,* vol. I, p. 378.
81. *The Western Monthly Magazine and Literary Journal,* vol. I, no. 3, April 1837, p. 208.   82. Mott, *op. cit.,* vol. I, p. 663.

Cincinnati's position. Ambitious western towns sent forth abortive attempts at magazine literature: *Western Ladies' Casket* of Concordsville, Indiana lasted at least six months; Dayton's *Western Miscellany*, a year; Fort Wayne's *Western Plow Boy*, three months; *The Frontier Monthly* of Hastings, Minnesota, three months; and *The Chicago Magazine*, despite its introductory note, that "we believe failure was never wedded to Chicago" [83] endured but four months. The West made a valiant effort; but it, like the South, was forced to acknowledge the leadership of Eastern magazines.

In dealing with ideas, however, place of publication was not necessarily important. There was sometimes a community of ideas which transcended geography. The editorials and comments in the magazines edited by the Methodist, Presbyterian, Unitarian and Universalist clergy were remarkably alike. The productions of the Moral Reform Societies could have had their covers changed and have been sent as an issue of the other society without surprising their readers. These were, of course, very specialized publications.

In the middle of the last century Boston, with her poets, historians, philosophers, and essayists was the hub of American literature.[84] New England held a dominance which was, at times, resented by champions of other sections. Yet, if it be true that attitudes are shaped in youth and early adulthood, then the preeminence of New England is extended to what most intellectual Bostonians of that day probably considered sub-literature—the fashion magazines. Mrs. Sarah Josepha Hale was past fifty when she left what many deemed to be the intellectual capital of the United States to become a literary light of Philadelphia and a leader in establishing the pattern for ladies' magazines. Mrs. Ann Stephens was from Connecticut and Mrs. Caroline Gilman, who edited *The Southern Rose* at Charleston, came from Boston. Mrs. Paulina Wright Davis, a liberal from Central New York, was a New Englander by adoption and Mrs. Caroline Dall was a Bostonian. While these transplanted New Englanders must have brought something of New England to the cities of their labor, they may easily have been influenced, in turn, by

83. *Chicago Magazine*, vol. I, no. 1, March 1857, p. 9.
84. Mott, *op. cit.*, vol. I, p. 378.

the intellectual climate of their adopted towns. The influence of New England in the ideas on education was, however, further accentuated; the two Barnards were trained at Yale and Mann at Brown and the three were New England born and bred.

The women editors naturally had not the formal education of many of the men. All were married, though Mrs. Hale was a widow when she added the duty of editor to that of home-maker. Except for Mrs. Swisshelm all were happy in their marriages. Even she, like the rest, had the encouragement of her husband in editing the *Pittsburgh Saturday Visiter.* These pioneers had the support of family and friends.

To what extent the ideas in these magazines influenced feminine America, it is difficult to say. No woman read them all. In fact, circulation statistics vary so remarkably that any estimate of homes reached is at best uncertain. How many women read the ladies' magazines is a matter of conjecture. How often they dipped into the *Atlantic* or *Harper's,* the *North American Review* or the *Southern Literary Messenger,* or any of the others, is equally problematic. At a time when there was little, if any, paid advertising, editors and publishers, if their magazines were to survive, must have been mindful of their readers. In the last analysis the subscriber held the purse strings and to a considerable extent controlled the output of the magazines.

Editors could, however, lead as well as follow opinion. All crusading journals were in the vanguard. Even Mrs. Hale in her editorial chit-chat in a fashion magazine sponsored many causes. Chief among them was education, which she brought to the attention of her readers in lengthy articles and in sugar-coated pills. She could begin with almost anything and conclude with education. A discussion of the sewing machine led her circuitously to the need for a high school for girls.[85] Every editor used "selections" to voice his own opinion. These were set in unexpected places and sometimes were printed in finer type so that they had the same appeal for the eye of the reader that an advertisement has, when dummied beside a column of print.

85. *Godey's Lady's Book,* vol. XLVII, no. 1, July 1853, p. 84.

There was more than one way to propagandize. Whether by intent or accident, many of the "fillers" in all the magazines dealt with education. There they were, often in the smallest type. Read or unread we have no way of knowing, yet they must have reached a far larger public than the professional journals of education. These ideas are of interest today in that they indicate what was available for the house-wife and mother.

CHAPTER TWO

What Is Education?

THERE was scarcely an editor—male or female—in the mid-nineteenth century who did not discuss education. All had or assumed to have a philosophical basis for their dictums. Some of the definitions were so broad as to include "everything"; others were statements of philosophy; a few confined education to training for citizenship. The writers tried to make clear their goals, their hopes, their dreams. Different points of view were presented in varying issues of a magazine; sometimes in the same issue, even in the same article. On the other hand, ideas were frequently repeated in several magazines and at intervals of decades. Nor were differences apparent between the ideas in ladies' magazines and general periodicals. There was a similarity in the aims of education as stated in the professionally edited educational journals and in the popular periodicals. These statements of belief formed a mosaic of the educational creeds to which educators and laymen gave allegiance during the period, 1830–1860. For purposes of clarity, these definitions have been grouped according to idea.

Education is life. Said the editor of *Godey's Lady's Book,* "Everything is education—the trains of thought you are indulging in this hour; the society in which you will spend the evening; the conversations, walks and incidents of tomorrow." [1] Mrs. Hale in her first article in *The Ladies' Magazine* [2] had presented this point of view and she held steadfastly to it throughout her career as an editor. Most of her brother and sister editors subscribed to this belief. They, too, recognized that in such a concept of education their magazines had a definite place. They were not so frank as Mrs. Hale, who boldly

1. *Godey's Lady's Book,* vol. LVI, no. 3, March 1858, p. 283.
2. *The Ladies' Magazine,* vol. I, no. 1, January 1828, pp. 1–3.

stated that it was "this public enthusiasm in the cause of education which encourages the numerous aspirants for fame and profit to send forth their periodicals in every form that fancy can devise to attract, and under every name that ingenuity can discover to allure." [3] Even those editors whose greatest financial ambition seems to have been to pay the printer agreed that education could "very properly be used to describe every effort and action of our entire life," [4] that "every new thought, every act we witness, or word we hear spoken, helps to form our education." [5] There is, however, an important difference in the meaning of "life," for to writers steeped in the theology of the time, it included life hereafter as well as life on earth.

This attitude toward life leads to the second concept of education, moral education with a view to life celestial. "Our whole life is a school, in which it is designed for us to prepare for a higher and eternal system of education, to be forever perfected by good men and angels, aye even by the Great God himself." [6] A writer in the *Ladies' Companion* mistrusted the kind of education then prevalent; he felt that "as men are now educated, they can neither understand or believe anything." [7] For years the magazines edited by clergymen stressed the necessity for religious education and discipline. Education was religious and moral as well as physical and scientific. [8] It was "the entire training of the entire capacities from birth onward and upward." [9] This belief in the value of moral education was not confined to the magazines edited by the clergy. Edward D. Mansfield in "Modern Education" pointed out that it was impossible to effect any moral reform by "mere *mental* instruction," [10] and a writer in the *Lady's Book* noted that while the infants of savages and civilized men were the same, the adults differed because of the kind of education they received. [11] To Timothy Flint, writing in *Knickerbocker's*

3. *Ibid.,* p. 1.   4. *The Una,* vol. II, no. 5, May 1854, p. 264.
5. *The Lily,* vol. V, No. 17, September 1, 1853, p. 2.   6. *Ibid.*
7. *Ladies' Companion,* vol. 20 (new series vol. I), no. 2, June 1844, p. 95.
8. *The Universalist and Ladies' Repository,* vol. 10, no. 6, November 1841, p. 235.
9. *Southern Lady's Companion,* vol. 5, no. 6, September 1851, p. 156.
10. *Southern Quarterly Review,* vol. XXVII (new series vol. XI), April 1855, pp. 451–476, especially p. 455.
11. *Godey's Lady's Book,* vol. XXI, no. 3, September 1840, p. 107.

on "The influence of Education on the Formation of Character," character was determined by "temperament, endowment, and education." It was the function of education to "modify the original endowment." [12] Educators, too, were told that "the teacher's great function" was to "develop the whole living being." [13] The student should be "taught his whole duty to himself, his fellows and his God —the consequence of obedience and disobedience—that virtue is the only road to true fame and that the intellectual and virtuous soul only can realize permanent happiness." [14]

Education should be functional. A. G., writing in *The Free Enquirer,* felt that "education should embrace the practice, no less than the theory of science, that it should lead to the observation of the facts of which learning treats;—and inculcate the moral principle out of which manners grow." [15] In "Modern Ideas Concerning Education," a satire on what professors teach, the writer made clear that to "profess" did not necessarily mean to "know." [16] Another writer in a much later issue of the same magazine (*Southern Literary Messenger*) inquired why it was that "amidst all our educational advantages we have so few educated men." [17] Joseph Omrod, Esq. in articles on "Intellectual Discipline and the Schools" pointed out the desirability of teaching from objects as well as from books. He described the work of an "ingenious German, named Pestalozzi, [who] being strongly impressed with the little efficiency of the common modes of instruction by means of the book only, devised a system which he carried into effect under the names of 'Lessons on Objects.' " [18] A broader aspect of functional education was thus recognized.

12. *The Knickerbocker,* vol. II, no. 6, December 1833, pp. 401–409 (quotation p. 407).

13. *Common School Journal,* vol. I, no. 4, February 15, 1839, pp. 56–62 (quotation p. 57—Report of Common School Committee).

14. *Monthly Literary Miscellany, a Compendium of Literary, Philosophical and Religious Knowledge,* vol. VI, no. V, May 1852, pp. 213–215 (quotation p. 215).

15. *Free Enquirer,* vol. 4, no. 8, December 17, 1831, p. 62 (article pp. 62–63).

16. *Southern Literary Messenger,* vol. VII, no. 10, October 1842, pp. 625–628.

17. *Ibid.,* vol. XXVIII, no. 4, April 1859, pp. 307–310.

18. *The Western Journal of Agriculture, Manufacture, Mechanic Arts,*

Education is training for citizenship.[19] An article in *Frazier's Magazine* attributed the prosperity of America to the "general enlightenment" of her people.[20] The value of free education as preparation for citizenship was shown in a learned article, "Education in Virginia," [21] while "Free Schools and the University of Virginia" [22] in a later issue of the *Southern Literary Messenger* is based on the sound political maxim of Lord Brougham, "Education is the cheapest defense of a nation." [23] To Mrs. Jane Swisshelm, it was the basis of all public reform and consequently of desirable citizenship. In her editorial, "Common Schools," she asked, ". . . What is the use of writing to people who cannot read? . . . Education is the only means that can make men approximate to the state of equality which philanthropists and reformers dream over. Nothing but education can elevate the masses. . . ." [24]

Education helps to prevent delinquency.[25] Evidence was given to show there were more criminals who could not read and write than those who could.[26]

Education is the means of perpetuating culture. To Mrs. Stephens, writing in *Peterson's,* culture was "the product of social and moral causes, as well as intellectual ones," [27] and was passed on to successive generations by means of education. It is interesting to note how broad her conception of culture was.

Internal Improvement, Commerce and General Literature, vol. II, no. V, May 1849, pp. 324–333; vol. III, no. II, November 1849, pp. 117–129 (quotation p. 118).

19. *DeBow's Review and Industrial Resources, Statistics, etc.,* vol. XVIII, o.s., vol. I, n.s., no. III, March 1855, p. 415; *Western Monthly Magazine,* vol. III, no. XIII, January 1834, pp. 30–35.

20. Quoted in *Harper's New Monthly Magazine,* vol. I, no. II, July 1850, p. 209.

21. *Southern Literary Messenger,* vol. VII, no. 9, September 1841, pp. 631–637.

22. *Ibid.,* vol. XX, no. 2, February 1854, pp. 65–75.   23. *Ibid.,* p. 65.

24. *Pittsburgh Saturday Visiter,* vol. III, no. 11, March 30, 1850, p. 42.

25. *DeBow's Review and Industrial Resources, Statistics, etc.,* vol. XVIII, o.s., vol. I, n.s., March 1855, pp. 409–421; *Friend of Virtue,* vol. XI, no. 11, June 1, 1848, p. 175.

26. *The Western Journal of Agriculture, Manufacture, Mechanic Arts, Internal Improvement, Commerce and General Literature,* vol. IV, no. VI, September 1851, pp. 359–365 (entire article pp. 356–367).

27. *Peterson's Magazine,* vol. XXXVIII, no. 5, November 1860, p. 402.

Education may be informal, and often that which is almost un-conscious on the part of the educator is the most lasting. In "Editorial Chit-Chat," the editor of *Graham's Magazine* conversed with parents on their important role. ". . . They [parents] educate their children to a certain extent whether they will or not. The mind of every child is influenced by the grown people around them, and after teaching never destroys or effaces these early memories. How important, then, that they should be good ones. . . ." [28]

Education should be forward looking. Ada Clare, writing on prejudices in her column, "Thoughts and Things," made this point succinctly. ". . . The father's experience, his guidance, his advice is most excellent for the son, but it is only to teach him to go forward. The father must learn that he must look onward with the son; the son cannot look backward with him. . . ." [29]

The purpose of education is to form habits. The *Southern Rose Bud* presented this idea by means of a conundrum. "Why is education like a tailor? [30] . . . Answer— Because it forms our habits." [31]

Education helps the individual to develop into a well-rounded person physically, mentally, morally, spiritually.[32] "The word literally means to draw out, to develop, and may very properly be used to describe every effort and action of our entire life; for, as we are designed for personal growth and progress, every act which we perform, whether of the body or mind, is at once achievement and discipline. . . ." [33] "Education, in the widest sense signifies the development, discipline, and cultivation of all powers and faculties of man, physical, mental and moral." [34] G. V. H. Forbes twenty years

28. *Graham's Illustrated Magazine of Literature, Romance, Art and Fashion,* vol. XLIX, no. 2, August 1856, p. 175.

29. *New York Saturday Press,* vol. III, no. 9, March 3, 1860, p. 2.

30. *Southern Rose Bud,* vol. 2, no. 44, June 28, 1834, p. 175.

31. *Ibid.,* vol. 2, no. 45, July 5, 1834, p. 179.

32. *Western Literary Messenger, a Family Magazine of Literature, Science, Art, Morality and General Intelligence,* vol. XV, no. 4, December 1850, p. 159.

33. *The Una,* vol. II, no. 5, May 1854, p. 264; the same idea was given by the editor (George Brewster) in "Etymology of Education" in *The Western Literary Magazine and Journal of Education, Science, Art, and Morals* (Columbus, 1851; Cleveland, 1854), pp. 77–80.

34. *Southern Quarterly Review,* vol. XIX (new series vol. I), no. 1, April 1856, pp. 168–188 (entire article) p. 170 (quotation).

earlier in *The Ladies' Garland* had stated much the same idea;[35] a few months later the editor quoted to the same effect "that excellent writer Dr. Channing." [36] Joseph Omrod, Esq.[37] and other writers in *Gleason's* [38] and the *Western Monthly* [39] shared this opinion.

Education should be graded to suit the development of the child. Children should not be hurried from one study to another, from one grade to another. "Each gradation of the study is reached before the faculty of the mind which is necessary to the prosecution of it. . . . The first period of mental development is the period of fancy and imagination, the second of memory and the third of reason." [40] It seems as if the writer thought education applied only to the mind. Another writer made the same point even more clearly in the *Common School Assistant*. The main object of education he considered to be "the development and discipline of the human mind." [41] R. C. in the *Free Enquirer* described education as a "cerebral excitement" carried on all through life.[42]

Perhaps the most inclusive statement on education was made in the "Editor's Table" of *Harper's*. In it were included all the ideas prevalent throughout the period. It clearly showed, however that education was general and cultural, that it trained the whole man.

What is Education?

On this question every man feels at home . . . The answers are almost innumerable—education is useful knowledge—it is practical training for all pursuits of life—it is culture—it is growth—it is discipline—it is learning to think—it is learning to act—it is *educing* the statue from the block of marble—it is the development of the mind and body—the development of the whole man, physically, mentally, morally—it is preparation for business, for success in life,

35. *The Ladies' Garland,* vol. I, no. 5, July 15, 1837, p. 75.

36. *Ibid.,* vol. I, no. 9, October 7, 1837, p. 135.

37. *The Western Journal of Agriculture, Manufacture, Mechanic Arts, Internal Improvement, Commerce and General Literature,* vol. II, no. III, March 1849, pp. 168–175 (especially p. 168).

38. *Gleason's Pictorial Drawing Room Companion,* vol. IV, no. 7, whole no. 85, February 12, 1853, p. 107.

39. *The Western Monthly,* vol. III, no. 8, February 1830, pp. 393–402.

40. *Southern Literary Messenger,* vol. XXVIII, no. 4, April 1859, pp. 307–310.

41. *Common School Assistant,* vol. II, no. 4, April 1837, pp. 26–27.

42. *Free Enquirer,* vol. V, no. 8, December 15, 1832, p. 62.

for working out the problems of humanity, &c., &c. May we not find one term that will embrace whatever of truth there is in these metaphors and yet exclude the error which may be regarded as attaching more or less to each one of them. . . . Education then, aims at the HEALTH OF THE SOUL, the production of a sound mind. . . .

The true idea, then, of education is catholic, in distinction from what is partial in human pursuit. It is that which pertains to man, *as man*, in distinction from what belongs to him as a farmer, a mechanic, a lawyer, an engineer or a merchant. It embraces not the trades, the businesses, but the humanities.[43]

At a time when there was a farm available for every young man (the Preemption Act, whereby a squatter could secure title to 160 acres by paying a minimum price, was passed in 1841), and when growing industry offered work to all, there was no formal vocational education. The need, however, for training "a daughter to some useful occupation" in order that she might not be destitute, if she should become a widow, was stressed.[44] It was felt that education would make a boy a better farmer; but the writer made clear that he meant a cultural education and not specific training in the art of husbandry.[45]

The value of such a cultural education was frequently stressed.[46] "The possession of knowledge" was deemed "its own reward." [47]

Underlying all the concepts of education was stated or implied the belief that the ultimate goal of all education was the attainment of a fine ethical character. This ethical character was deemed the directing force in life, the basis of citizenship and of all activity. Thus the philosophy of education was rooted in the religious concepts of the time. Since the religious concepts remained much the same,

43. *Harper's New Monthly Magazine,* vol. V, no. XXV, June 1852, pp. 122–126.
44. *The Western Casket,* vol. V, no. I, January 1853, pp. 14–16 (quoted from the *Saturday Gazette*).
45. *Western Plow Boy,* vol. I, no. 1, January 1, 1853, pp. 3–4; no. 6, March 15, 1853, pp. 61–63.
46. *Frontier Monthly,* vol. I, no. 2, May 1859, pp. 61–62; *The Oak Leaf,* vol. I, no. 4, January 1857, pp. 120–122.
47. *United States Magazine and Democratic Review,* vol. XVII, no. LXXXV, July 1845, pp. 40–50.

the philosophy of education was unchanging. Yet the concrete expression of this philosophy did change, as it was modified by the events of the day. Training for citizenship became prominent in the 1840's, because the extension of suffrage made the need apparent. The ideal education, however, remained the same—the development of a fine person through general or cultural education.

CHAPTER THREE

The Importance of Female Education

No aspect of education was more discussed a century ago than that of female education. It was even the subject of a Phi Beta Kappa address which Professor Silliman made before the society at Yale. He remarked that the best diploma for a woman was a large family and a happy husband and that "He" should be placed before the "Arts" in the degree of "Mistress of Arts," thus making "Mistress of Hearts." [1] Professor Silliman was unique among educators in that he so enthusiastically endorsed woman's sphere. By educators her sphere was usually ignored; her education desired.

To the writers in the popular periodicals, however, both woman's sphere and her education were subjects of debate. The debate was waged with many of the same arguments in 1860 as in 1830, in the magazines for ladies as in the popular periodicals. The debate centered about three focal questions: What was woman's sphere? Could her mind be educated? Was it equal to that of man? Each question and the answer thereto had a direct bearing upon the others. There were enough shades of opinion and niceties of distinction to provide preachers, commencement orators, and masculine writers for magazines, as well as the women themselves who dared to express their hopes and ambitions, with more than ample material.

The traditional conviction that woman's sphere was the home fixed her education within narrow limits.[2] As the number of tasks in the home decreased with the progress of the industrial revolution,

---

1. *Western Plow Boy,* vol. I, no. 3, February 1, 1853, p. 48.
2. Thomas Woody, *A History of Women's Education in the United States* (The Science Press, Lancaster, Pa., 1929, 2 vols.) vol. 1, chapters 1–6.

woman's range of activity contracted. With improvement in her husband's financial status, it further contracted until at times, except for occasional supervision, even the kitchen and the nursery were out of her sphere. A lady who presided in the drawing-room needed accomplishments to display—a little French to inject into conversation, the ability to accompany herself, while she sang a sentimental song or two, a bit of useless handiwork to create the impression of busyness. Most women and girls got their ideals of a lady from the wives and daughters of the well-to-do, either in real life or in fiction. By the middle of the nineteenth century, their sphere was centered in the parlor. It was in the parlor, too, that a gentleman courted his lady. The novels and the stories led every girl and her mother to believe that, regardless of any lack of wealth, a gentleman would wish the one whom he would select to be his bride to be a lady. At a time when there was only one generally accepted criterion for feminine success, the effect on the education of girls was unmistakable. Finishing schools flourished.

None of the editors espoused the cause of "finishing," yet the vehemence with which they attacked it,[3] the continued presence of "accomplishments" in the curricula of the schools for young ladies,[4] as well as many of the stories, suggest that "finishing" was the accepted mode of education. Even in attacking accomplishments, writers of stories made them attractive to girls. Throughout the year 1843, "Celia Howard, or the Young Lady Who Had Finished Her Education" by T. S. Arthur was featured in *Miss Leslie's Magazine*. The fortunes of Celia "who couldn't cook, make her clothes, teach her younger brothers and sisters or earn money" were traced "in the three conditions of maiden, wife and mother." While it was quite apparent that Celia would have had a much easier time in marriage if she had learned to cook and sew when single, it was equally apparent that Celia, through the aid of her "accomplishments" was

3. *Godey's Lady's Book*, vol. XLV, no. 3, September 1852, pp. 273–274; *Ladies' Pearl*, vol. II, no. 11, May 1842, p. 252; *Harper's New Monthly Magazine*, vol. XV, no. LXXXIX, October 1857, pp. 674–678.
4. *Godey's Lady's Book*, vol. XLVII, no. 1, July 1853, p. 85; vol. L, no. 4, April 1855, p. 369; vol. LI, no. 5, November 1855, p. 469; vol. LIV, no. 3, March 1857, p. 275; vol. LVI, no. 4, April 1858, p. 373.

successful by the standard of the 1840's.[5] Mary Davenant in "Fanny's Fine Education"[6] was less ambiguous in attacking accomplishments, but her story was prosy. The cleverest exposé of the folly and harm of finishing schools was that illuminating but lengthy satirical "poem" describing the school of Madame Cancan, with "her morals infernal, her manners elysian." In the pursuit of fashion, it was shown, morals were forgotten and the effect was as harmful to society as to the pupil, Mary Degai. Yet Madame Cancan continued her work despite the wrecks she had caused.[7] The spirit of the satire is given in the conclusion.

> Madame Cancan still lives and still ogles and teaches,
> And still her lay sermons on Fashions she preaches;
> Still keeps of smooth phrases the choisest assortment;
> Still lectures on dress, easy carriage, deportment;
> And spends all her skill in thus moulding her pets
> Into very-genteelly-got-up marionettes.
> Yes! Puppet's the word; for there's nothing inside
> But a clock-work of vanity, fashion and pride!
> Puppets warranted sound, that without any falter
> When wound up will go—just as far as the altar;
> But when once the cap's donned with the matronly border,
> Lo! the quiet machine goes at once out of order.[8]

To combat this concept of woman's sphere and miseducation, the editors struggled valiantly. To some the accomplishments were "a gilded cheat"[9] and they had naught but contempt for the "useful women" brought up to be "men catchers."[10] To the writer on "Uneducated Women" in the *Common School Journal*, "a mother whose maiden days were devoted to the acquirement of fashionable

5. *Miss Leslie's Magazine*, vol. I, January 1843, pp. 19–22; February 1843, pp. 65–69; March 1843, pp. 92–96; April 1843, pp. 132–135; May 1843, pp. 167–170; June 1843, pp. 203–206; vol. 2, July 1843, pp. 18–20; August 1843, pp. 39–43; September 1843, pp. 73–76; October 1843, pp. 110–112; November 1843, pp. 163–167; December 1843, pp. 197–200.

6. *Ladies' National Magazine*, vol. X, no. 1, July 1846, pp. 25–31.

7. *Harper's New Monthly Magazine*, vol. XVII, no. CX, September 1858, pp. 435–445.

8. *Ibid.*, p. 445.

9. *Home Journal,* whole no. 620, series for 1857, no. 52, December 26, 1857, p. 2.

10. *Ladies' Companion,* vol. 3, no. 1, May 1835, p. 32.

accomplishments, to the exclusion of solid mental culture and ac-
quirements was ignorant." [11] Mrs. Hale suggested that accomplishments might have their use but they should not be the "alpha and
omega of the entire educational routine." [12] Woman's sphere was
the home, but it should be all the home, not simply the drawing-
room. To think of education as something apart from domestic life,
as incompatible with it, was considered by Mrs. Hale to be as false
as religion was often represented to be with relation to innocent
pleasure.[13] To some writers the person best suited to give such
instruction was the mother of a family in her home.[14] To Catharine
Beecher, however, instruction should not be confined to the home,
but given at school as well.[15] Domestic economy should be a most
important subject in a girl's education [16] and her "business training"
should include enough book-keeping and arithmetic to enable her to
manage a household.[17] Women writers stressed the practical aspects
of the training for this phase of her sphere.

Most of the men and many of the women were interested in that
other important aspect of her sphere—the training of children.
These middle-aged, perhaps even elderly folk, in the middle of the
last century turned for inspiration to those in whom they had found
complete security in childhood—their mothers. The mother, who had
received her training at the turn of the century or even in the eighteenth century was a very different person from the product of the
finishing school; and the memory of her influence, hallowed through
the intervening years, became the ideal which commencement orators [18] and preachers [19] held before their feminine listeners and

11. *Common School Journal*, vol. IX, no. 19, October 1, 1847, pp. 297–
298 (quotation p. 298).
12. *Godey's Lady's Book*, vol. LI, no. 5, November 1855, p. 401.
13. *Ladies' Magazine*, vol. IV, no. IV, April 1831, p. 148.
14. *Ibid.*, pp. 145–154.
15. *Ladies' Garland*, vol. VII, new series, vol. I, no. 10, April 1844, pp.
227–228.
16. See Chapter IV.
17. *Southern Lady's Companion*, vol. III, no. 4, July 1849, pp. 92–95.
18. *Southern Lady's Companion*, vol. II, no. 5, August 1848, pp. 112–115,
"Extract from an Address Delivered at the Commencement of the Weslyan
Female College," Macon, Georgia, by the Hon. Robert M. Charlton.
19. *Ibid.*, vol. III, no. 9, December 1849, pp. 204–206. The need for
"correct Christian principles" to "carry (her) through the dubious voyage

editors placed before their readers.[20] This idealized mother was crystallized by a theology which placed first high moral values and a rewarding heaven.

It was generally accepted that woman was morally superior to man. Was not Adam "made out of dust refined" and "Eve out of dust doubly refined"?[21] Woman's profession, according to Catharine Beecher was "to form immortal minds, and to watch, to nurse, to rear the bodily system so fearfully and wonderfully made and upon which the health and well-being of the mind so greatly depends."[22] The importance of the work of the mother was shown in learned articles[23] and in biographical sketches[24] such as those of Washington's mother,[25] and the mother on the frontier.[26] The writer in *The Lily* gave a different slant to the measure of the work of the Pilgrim Mothers.

The Pilgrim Fathers, forsooth! What had they to endure in comparison with the Pilgrim Mothers? It is true that they had hunger and cold and sickness and danger—foes without and foes within—but the

---

of life" was stressed. *Ibid.,* vol. V, no. 5, August 1851, pp. 121–124. Bishop Andrew believed that "it was an acknowledged truth that the influence of mothers was more powerful than that of fathers" (p. 121).

20. *Ibid.,* vol. V, no. 10, January 1852, pp. 301–302 quoted Daniel Webster; *Ladies' Companion,* vol. IX, no. 8, October 1838, pp. 293–296.

21. *Southern Rose,* vol. 7, no. 21, June 8, 1839, p. 329.

22. *Southern Lady's Companion,* vol. II, no. 5, August 1848, p. 116.

23. *Ladies' Companion,* vol. IX, no. 8, October 1838, pp. 293–296; *Ladies' Garland,* vol. I, no. 4, June 3, 1837, p. 61; *Philadelphia Album and Ladies' Literary Gazette,* vol. II, no. 1, June 6, 1827, p. 15; no. 3, June 23, 1827, p. 23; ("On Female Education" by A. G. Thomas, Esq. of Edgefield Court House, South Carolina, awarded prize of fifty dollars by *Philadelphia Album*) especially p. 15.

24. *Godey's Lady's Book,* vol. XXXVII, no. 4, October 1848, pp. 201–202; no. 5, November 1848, pp. 263–265; no. 6, December 1848, pp. 372–375; vol. XXXVIII, no. 5, May 1849, pp. 307–308; vol. XXXIX, no. 1, July 1849, pp. 28–30; no. 2, August 1849, pp. 115–116; no. 4, October 1849, pp. 251–252; no. 6, December 1849, pp. 444–448; vol. XL, no. 3, March 1850, pp. 181–187; no. 4, April 1850, pp. 257–261; vol. XLI, no. 4, October 1850, pp. 201–204; vol. XLIX, no. 3, September 1859, pp. 224–229. Sketches of "Women of the Revolution" by Mrs. Ellet.

25. *Ladies' Magazine,* vol. IV, no. IX, September 1831, p. 385.

26. *Godey's Lady's Book,* vol. XLII, no. 1, January 1851, pp. 43–47; vol. XLIV, no. 1, January 1852, pp. 71–75; no. 4, April 1852, pp. 266–268.

unfortunate Pilgrim Mothers! They had not only these to endure,
but they had the Pilgrim Fathers! [27]

To many of the writers in the decades before the Civil War the
concept of woman as wife was an extension and glorification of
woman as mother.[28] Was not her influence exerted upon "the character of men and the destiny of our rising nation," [29] just as she was
"the mother of future statesmen"? [30] Since woman's influence was
so great, she should be educated. Writers marshalled their arguments.[31] "The future usefulness and happiness of her children depended mostly upon the early training of the infant mind." [32] Because
a mother's influence was so much greater than that of a father, girls
should, if necessary, be educated even at the expense of boys.[33] A
writer on the Choctaw Indians presented much the same idea as may
be seen from this statement:

When I lived among the Choctaw Indians, I held consultation with
one of their chiefs respecting the successive stage of their progress
in civilized life; and among other things he informed me, that at the
first start they fell into a great mistake—they only sent their boys to
school. These boys became intelligent men, but they married uneducated and uncivilized wives and the uniform result was that the
children were all like the mothers. Thus the father lost all his interest in both wife and children. "And now," said he, "if we could
educate but one class of our children, we should choose the girls, for,
when they become mothers, they will educate their sons." [34]

27. *The Lily,* vol. V, no. 14, July 15, 1853, p. 112.
28. *Ladies' Garland,* vol. II, no. 1, July 1844, pp. 23–25; *Ladies' Magazine,*
vol. IV, no. III, March 1831, pp. 139–140; *Godey's Lady's Book,* vol. XLIV,
no. 6, June 1852, pp. 511–515; *Southern Lady's Companion,* vol. II, no. 5,
August 1848, pp. 112–115; no. 11, February 1849, pp. 249–250.
29. *Ladies' Pearl,* vol. II, no. 4, October 1841, pp. 76–79.
30. *Ladies' Companion,* vol. 8, November 1837, p. 18.
31. *Ibid.,* vol. IX, no. 7, September 1838, pp. 232–235; *Ibid.,* vol. XIII,
no. 6, September 1840, pp. 245–246; *Ladies' Magazine,* vol. III, no. III,
March 1830, pp. 105–115; vol. IV, no. VI, June 1831, pp. 256–269; *Godey's
Lady's Book,* vol. XXI, no. 1, July 1840, p. 34.
32. *Godey's Lady's Book,* vol. XX, no. 2, February 1840, pp. 92–93.
33. *Southern Lady's Companion,* vol. V, no. 5, August 1851, p. 121.
34. *The Sibyl,* vol. 1, no. 19, April 1, 1857, p. 146; quoted from *Prairie
Farmer.*

The influence of women upon their contemporaries was also noted. Had not Cato said, "Romans govern the world, but it is the women who govern the Romans"? [35] A nineteenth-century woman insisted that "When women are well informed, men dare not be ignorant." [36] One editor felt an educated wife made a more desirable companion and a better mother.[37]

While there was agreement that woman should not simply be educated to "dress and catch a beau," [38] there was none on the kind of education she should receive. This depended on whether "the female minds are as susceptible of intellectual culture as those that reside in a stronger wrought tenement of bone and sinew." [39] A few courageous men—J. G. Haswell,[40] H. W. Bellows,[41] Thomas Wentworth Higginson,[42] Luther Lee,[43] and Sidney Smith,[44] answered in the affirmative and one even suggested that there was "no sex in mind." [45]

Few writers were so bluntly frank as the one who said, "The great argument against the existence of this equality of intellect in woman is, that it does not exist" [46] or another who noted that "the Goddess of Wisdom sprung from the head of Jove, a proof that she has but few relations on the female side." [47] Only slightly less harsh was

35. *Godey's Lady's Book,* vol. LVI, no. 1, January 1858, p. 21.

36. *Southern Rose,* vol. 7, no. 12, February 2, 1839, p. 183.

37. *The Lady's World of Fashion,* vol. 1, no. 5, May 1842, pp. 156–157. The same idea is given in the *Register,* quoted in *Pittsburgh Saturday Visiter,* vol. III, no. 51, December 28, 1850, p. 200.

38. *The Sibyl,* vol. 1, no. 2, July 15, 1856, p. 16.

39. *Ladies' Pearl,* vol. II, no. 4, October 1841, pp. 76–79.

40. *Ladies' Repository,* vol. XIII, no. 8, August 1853, pp. 366–368.

41. *National Anti-Slavery Standard,* vol. II, no. 47, April 28, 1842, p. 188.

42. *The Atlantic Monthly,* vol. III, no. XVI, February 1859, pp. 137–150, copied in its entirety in *The Sibyl,* vol. III, no. 15, February 1, 1859, pp. 497–499; vol. III, no. 16, February 15, 1859, pp. 505–507; vol. III, no. 17, March 1, 1859, pp. 519–520. The authorship is established in *Atlantic Essays* by Thomas Wentworth Higginson (Boston, James P. Osgood and Company, 1871) pp. 93–153.

43. *Ladies' Pearl,* vol. II, no. 4, October 1841, pp. 76–79.

44. *Godey's Lady's Book,* vol. LI, no. 5, November 1855, pp. 401–403.

45. *National Anti-Slavery Standard,* vol. II, no. 47, April 28, 1842, p. 188 (H. W. Bellows).

46. Quoted from *The Saturday Review* in *Littell's Living Age,* vol. 64, no. 816, 21 January 1860, p. 184.

47. *Ladies' Companion,* vol. 4, December 1835, p. 86.

Fenelon, who used woman's inferiority to show her need for education; "Women in general have feebler minds than men; the weaker the mind is, the more important to fortify it." [48] Most of the writers, however, discussed woman's intellect from various angles and made very careful distinctions. One of the earliest of these discussions was "Selected Dialogue on Female Education between Theodosius and Eugenius" which opaquely lumbered through the broad-minded, femininely edited *National Magazine or Ladies Emporium.*[49]

Generally the ladies' magazines were loathe to accept the mental inferiority of the sex. Women's minds were simply "different." Mrs. Sigourney in "The Comparative Intellect of the Sexes" stated rather neatly the position of the group which recognized this difference but urged woman to develop her own sphere: "This subject, though often the theme of discussion, has been seldom candidly investigated. . . ." After citing evidence for several pages, she continued, "We arrive, therefore, at this conclusion. The sexes are intended for different spheres and constructed in conformity to their respective destinies. . . . But *disparity* does not *necessarily* imply inferiority. . . ." [50]

Men joined women in pointing out the differences between the male and the female mind. Women had "a natural gift of speech in greater perfection." [51] "The mind of a woman is more fluid as it were, than that of a man; it moves more easily and its operations have a less cohesive and permanent character." [52] Henry F. Harrington stated, "Woman has not the vigor and depth of thought, the accuracy of analysis, and the fidelity of judgment which are characteristic of man; and which seem to indicate his peculiar fitness to direct the helm of society. . . . Woman is not a lower creation. . . . She hath in an eminent degree intenser affections, loftier sentiments, a deeper love of the pure and the gentle and the virtuous. . . ." [53]

One editor who admitted that the mind of woman was equal to that

48. *Godey's Lady's Book,* vol. XLV, no. 3, September 1852, p. 273.
49. *National Magazine and Ladies' Emporium,* vol. I, no. 1, November 1830, pp. 21–25.
50. *Ladies' Magazine,* vol. III, no. VI, June 1830, pp. 241–245.
51. *Ladies' Miscellany,* vol. 1, no. 2, June 6, 1829, p. 5.
52. *Littell's Living Age,* vol. 49, no. 755, third series no. 33, 13 November 1858, pp. 483–499 (quotation p. 486).
53. *Ladies' Companion,* vol. IX, no. 7, September 1838, pp. 232–235.

of man hastened to add, ". . . But although the equality of woman is admitted on all hands, it does not follow that her sphere is the same as that of man. . . . It is no more the business of woman to lead our armies, to vote at the ballot box, or to wrangle on a public rostrum, than it is for a man to darn her stockings, nurse children or superintend a kitchen. . . . Educate her not only to be a graceful and accomplished being but a help-mate and a wife. . . ." [54]

A few inspired souls saw woman as a human being, entirely apart from any sphere. To them woman's mind, like man's, was capable of growth, and, like a man, she should be given the opportunity. [55] "The intrinsic value of the human mind," wrote "Ann" of "Port Byron" in *The Lily*, "and its infinite capacity for improvement, are the true reasons for its cultivation in woman no less than man. The first reason for the education of every mind should be its own development. We are too much inclined to urge the enlightenment of women, as a sure means of improving man, rather than as in itself an intrinsic excellence, with the conviction that every mind should be educated for its own development." [56] A more lengthy article in *The Dial*,[57] with greater erudition and with the transcendental philosophy, presented the same point of view and concluded, "Is this the ideal of a perfect woman, and if so, how does it differ from a perfect man?" [58]

As few thinkers, in a day long before modern psychology had individualized mentality, saw clearly that there was no sex in brains, so there were few women who dared to endeavor to cultivate their minds. Some of these seekers after mental development attained a result so different from what was deemed womanly and feminine that many of their sisters withdrew into their sphere; and pompous, foolish and ignorant men, "who being bound [as they thought] in

54. *The Lady's World of Fashion*, vol. 1, no. 5, May 1842, pp. 156–157.
55. *The Una*, vol. II, no. 11, November 1854, pp. 360–362, an article by Thomas Wentworth Higginson; see foot-note 42; *The Atlantic Monthly* vol. III, no. XVI, February 1859, pp. 137–150, and *The Sibyl*, vol. III, no. 15, February 1, 1859, pp. 497–499; no. 16, February 15, 1859, pp. 505–507, no. 17, March 1, 1859, pp. 519–526.
56. *The Lily*, vol. I, no. 5, May 1, 1849, p. 36.
57. *The Dial*, vol. I, no. III, January 1841, pp. 362–366.
58. *Ibid.*, p. 366.

point of sex, to know more, [were] not well pleased, in point of fact to know less," encouraged them to stay there. Neither these ladies nor gentlemen saw, as did the Reverend Sidney Smith, that all affectations and display proceeded from the supposition of possessing something better than the rest of the world possessed and that when knowledge was generally diffused among women, the conceit, which knowledge occasioned when rare, would be cured. The Reverend Mr. Smith hoped that woman could successfully cultivate her mind "without diminishing the gentleness and propriety of her manners." [59] In this way he bridged the gap between the ultra-feminist and the group who wished to extend her sphere gradually. If the concept of woman as mother were taken as the criterion, she could easily enlarge her sphere to influence children in the classroom, and as physician, to minister to the sick. If her moral superiority were taken as the standard, the study of theology was opened to her. Thus Mrs. Hale came to champion the causes of the female teacher [60] and physician,[61] and Mrs. Elizabeth Cady Stanton the study of divinity.[62]

Mrs. Paulina Wright Davis, who stood for the development of woman as a person, used the arguments of those who would limit her sphere for extending it in her "Report on the Education of Females" at the Worcester Convention.

By equality, we do not mean either identity or likeness, in general or in particulars, of the two sexes; but equivalence of dignity, necessity and use; admitting all differences and modifications which shall not affect a just claim to equal liberty in development and action. . . . Differences in moral and intellectual things, if regarded as antagonism to the extent of unlikeness, would render any consistent system of organization impossible. Thus, Woman, from her conceded superiority in the family affection would be entitled to the exclusive control of the domestic function; her higher and more susceptible religious constitution would give her a monopoly of the *priestly* office;

59. *Godey's Lady's Book,* vol. LI, no. 5, November 1855, pp. 401–403.
60. *Ibid.,* vol. XLV, no. 2, August 1852, p. 193; vol. XLVII, no. 1, July 1853, p. 84; vol. XLIV, no. 6, June 1852, pp. 511–515.
61. *Ibid.,* vol. L, no. 2, February 1855, p. 175.
62. *The Una,* vol. III, no. 9, September 1855, p. 140.

and her eminent moral endowments fit her for the rule of *social life*
and manners including all those municipal laws which regulate the
relations of men to each other in civil society. So that the professions
of Law, Theology and Medicine, in nearly all its branches, would
belong to her by right of special fitness, and the men by the same
rule would be wholly excluded. This principle of distribution would
leave—what would it leave the sole administration of men? Nothing
but the ordering of these affairs, and the cultivation of those sciences,
for which their ruder strength of muscle, greater bluntness of nerve
and firmer qualities of logical reasoning, if they have all these or
either of them qualify them. . . .[63]

No matter what the concept of woman's sphere, from the many
who, in practice, confined it to the parlor, to the few who aspired
to break all bonds asunder and let her have the same opportunities
as man, with all the shades of differences between these two extremes,
there was one point of agreement,—woman should be educated. To
many of these writers the education of woman was "one of the great
facts of the age, . . . a bold outstanding movement, full of significance, and worthy of challenge to all thinking people." [64] To
Mann, Barnard, and all the educational leaders of the time, there was
no question of woman's intelligence. They were interested in giving
her educational opportunities.[65] Consequently the discussion of her
sphere was carried on by orators and writers, husbands and wives,
and not by educators.

Not only did these writers and orators repeat arguments, they
even quoted the same article at intervals of decades.

No where is this more clearly shown than in the quotation of
the Reverend Sidney Smith's "Female Education." This article
which appeared, unsigned, in the *Edinburgh Review* in 1810, reviewed Thomas Broadhurst's *Advice to Young Ladies on the Improvement of the Mind,* which was published in London in 1808. It

63. *The Una,* vol. II, no. 11, November 1854, pp. 360–362.
64. *Harper's New Monthly Magazine,* vol. XV, no. XC, November 1857,
pp. 776–783. Quoted extensively in *The Sibyl,* vol. II, no. 13, January 1,
1858, pp. 294 ff. The sentence quoted is on p. 776 in *Harper's* and p. 294 in
The Sibyl.
65. Woody, *op. cit.,* vol. I, p. 90.

was quoted from the *Edinburgh Review* in the *Album and Ladies' Weekly Gazette* of Philadelphia in September 1826. Carey and Hart, Philadelphia publishers, included it in *The Works of the Reverend Sydney Smith,* in 1847. Mrs. Hale quoted this "first rate essay on the subject of female education," in the *Lady's Book* for November 1855; she further noted that in 1855 one did not frequently "hear objections to women being educated as rational and responsible beings," but that "the actual facts" fell "far short of the mark." [66]

In 1826, the article had been presented to the ladies of Philadelphia without any such introductory comment. Therein lay the progress made in the discussion of woman's sphere—not in the ideas presented, but in the way in which they were presented. By the 1850's, the need for the education of woman no matter what her sphere should be, was recognized. The answers to the questions "what she should be taught" and "where she should be educated" focused the debate on concrete problems, problems which were stormheads for discussions during the decades before the Civil War.

66. *The Album and Ladies' Weekly Gazette,* vol. I, no. XIV, September 6, 1826, pp. 1–2; no. XVI, September 20, 1826, pp. 2–3; *The Works of the Rev. Sydney Smith,* three volumes complete in one, Philadelphia, Carey and Hart, 1847, pp. 79–85; *Godey's Lady's Book,* vol. LI, no. 5, November 1855, pp. 401–403.

CHAPTER FOUR

Curricula for Young Ladies

W‌HAT should a young lady be taught? Indeed this was a challenge,—a challenge most difficult to meet because it was concrete. The interpretation of this challenge was, however, colored by the writer's attitude toward her sphere. There was no one even so early as 1820 who voiced objections to her need to know the three R's. Yet in practice it was often impossible for her to surmount the difficulties attendant upon the gaining of this modicum of knowledge.

To meet this problem, Mrs. Emma Willard founded Troy Seminary in 1821. In the work of educating girls, she was joined by such women as her sister, Mrs. Lincoln Phelps, Zilpah P. Grant and Mary Lyon. These women were not content to give their students minimum essentials. They wished them to have the same curriculum of culture as that given to boys. As that curriculum was broadened to include such subjects as modern languages, history, book-keeping, and physical education, women educators increased the opportunities for girls. Some of them included domestic economy in their offerings, for they recognized that most of their students would become home-makers.

At the same time that women educators were seeking enlarged opportunities for girls, realistic school-mistresses, in their desire to please parents and thus secure patrons, persisted in "finishing" a young lady. Even those who clung to "finishing" could not agree on a curriculum. Indeed one writer in 1837, the year Mount Holyoke was founded, said frankly he did not know what a young lady should be taught.[1]

1. *Ladies' Companion,* vol. 8, no. 1, November 1837, p. 19.

Others resorted to glittering generalities.[2] Still others gave the all inclusive "everything." Motte Hall presented the position of the last group in "poetry."

PLACING A DAUGHTER AT SCHOOL

I have brought my daughter to you to be taught everything

> "Dear madam, I've called for the purpose
>   Of placing my daughter at school;
> She's only thirteen, I assure you,
>   And remarkably easy to rule.
> I'd have her learn painting and music,
>   Gymnastics and dancing, pray do,
> Philosophy, grammar and logic,
>   You'll teach her to read, of course, too.
>
> "I wish her to learn every study
>   Mathematics are down on my plan,
> But of figures she scarce has an inkling
>   Pray instruct her in those, if you can.
> I'd have her taught Spanish and Latin,
>   Including the language of France;
> Never mind her very bad English,
>   Teach her that when you find a good chance.
>
> "On the harp she must be a proficient,
>   And play the guitar pretty soon,
> And sing the last opera music
>   Even though she can't turn a right tune.
> You must see that her manners are finished,
>   That she moves with a Hebe-like grace;
> For, though she is lame and one-sided,
>   That's nothing to do with the case.
>
> "Now to you I resign this young jewel,
>   And my words I would have you obey;
> In six months return her, dear madam,
>   Shining bright as an unclouded day.

2. *Southern Lady's Companion,* vol. III, no. 6, September 1849, pp. 133–135; no. 8, November 1849, pp. 169–173.

She's no aptness, I grant you for learning
And her memory oft seems to halt;
But, remember, if she's not accomplished
It will certainly be your fault." [3]

"Placing a Daughter at School," like the more famous account of
the school of Madame Cancan,[4] gives a rather clear picture of the
finishing school, with its painting and music, dancing and deportment, its smattering of French and Spanish, Latin and grammar,
philosophy and logic, and, if there were time, English and mathematics. The most illuminating part of the description, however, is
not the bill of fare but the time taken to devour the feast—six
months. Obviously the daughter would have either mental indiges-
tion or a mere talking knowledge of the things that were talked about.
Therein lies the crux of the indictment against the finishing schools:
their complete lack of thoroughness. A corollary to this skimming
of the surface was their misplaced emphasis,—their stress on show
rather than on basic values.

In a very real sense the private school for girls was "the lengthened
shadow" of its headmistress. If she were a Madame Cancan, with
"her morals infernal, manners elysian," the product would naturally
be a "genteelly-got-up marionette" who at best would be amoral. On
the other hand it was possible for a private school for girls with the
right kind of principal to give girls a fairly good education.

Such a school was Miss S. J. Hale's Boarding and Day School
for Young Ladies which flourished in Philadelphia in the late 1850's
and was closed in the year 1863 by the untimely death of Miss Sarah
Josepha Hale.[5] The subjects taught were English branches, French
and Latin, drawing and oil-painting; instruction was given in dancing and on the piano, harp and guitar, and in voice. Significantly in
the announcements references were given. These included Mrs. Emma
Willard, Troy, N.Y., in whose school Miss Hale was educated;
Mrs. Lincoln Phelps, Baltimore, Md.; Henry Vethaka, LL.D.,

3. *Godey's Lady's Book,* vol. XLVI, no. 5, May 1853, p. 457.
4. *Harper's New Monthly Magazine,* vol. XVII, no. CX, September 1858,
pp. 435–445.
5. Entriken, *op. cit.,* p. 123; *Godey's Lady's Book,* vol. LXVII, no. 2,
August 1863, pp. 148–149 (an obituary for Miss Hale).

Provost of the University of Pennsylvania, the Bishop of the Diocese of Pennsylvania, and Louis A. Godey, Esq., Philadelphia. "Pew rent at cost," which appeared in the notices, would indicate that Miss Hale was not a Madame Cancan, but one would hardly expect a daughter of such an arbiter of morals and manners to lack the virtues which her mother tried to inspire her readers to cultivate. Miss Hale insisted that her patrons pay in advance semi-annually for a year's work which began "the first Monday in September" and ended "the last Wednesday in June." [6] In view of such lack of insistence in advertisements of many schools, it would seem that other aspiring headmistresses lacked the financial backing necessary to independence. The private school flourished only as it had patrons. In a day when even the most broad-minded men thought of woman as wife or mother but rarely as daughter,[7] it was not to be expected that a shrewd business man—for financial success was the criterion for masculine success as was marriage for feminine—would invest any more money than necessary in a daughter's intellectual dowry.

Partly because private schools were so at the mercy of their patrons, Emma Willard in 1818 launched her campaign for either publicly supported or privately endowed seminaries for girls,[8] where they could be better taught and where they could learn more substantial subjects.[9] In this work, which lasted for decades, she was aided by her sister and other founders of seminaries, as Mary Lyon and Zilpah P. Grant, by Catharine Beecher and the American Women's Educational Association. The ladies' magazines kept their readers informed of the hopes and aspirations of the leaders as well as the development of schools.

6. *Godey's Lady's Book*, vol. LVI, no. 4, April 1858, p. 373.
7. Two exceptions to this policy should be noted. "Where Our Daughters Go to School," in *Harper's New Monthly Magazine*, vol. XV, no. LXXXIX, October 1857, pp. 674–678, is an essay which in a logical way shows the lack of value of the finishing school. "Our Daughters," in the same magazine, vol. XVI, no. XCI, December 1857, pp. 72–77, shows that the chief concern of a father for his daughter is what may happen to her, not what she may do.
8. Woody, *op. cit.*, vol. I, pp. 305 ff.; Stuart G. Noble, *A History of American Education* (New York, Farrar and Rinehart, 1938, pp. xv, 440) pp. 247 ff.
9. Noble, *op. cit.*, pp. 251 ff.

The two subjects whose addition to the curriculum the members of this group of educators stressed most were domestic economy and physical education. The ladies' magazines did their part in these campaigns. Almost uniformly the magazine writers saw domestic economy as the chief means of enabling woman to perform what they deemed to be the proper function of her sphere.[10] Even the crusading magazines [11] endorsed it, for they, too, saw the home as the center of a woman's life. To them, however, it was not the circumference as well.

The editors used four means of popularizing domestic economy. They wrote editorials about it.[12] A study of domestic economy would enable a woman to run the *one* house so well that "the family would love home and feel happy there." [13]

Second they quoted well-known authorities. Miss Sedgewick believed that "a young lady totally ignorant of domestic affairs is nearly as unfit to be an American wife and mother, as though she were lame in both feet and hands." [14] Miss Catharine Beecher stressed the value of domestic economy [15] and stated that she did not consider it "a mark of gentility to be careless about expense" but advised that girls not be taught to "try to beat down a shopkeeper." [16] That a girl should have enough arithmetic and book-keeping to manage a household was recommended by an unnamed authority.[17] Mrs. Lydia Maria Child stressed "the need for *home* education." [18]

Third, schools where domestic economy was taught were de-

10. *The Ladies' Pearl,* vol. II, no. 5, November 1841, p. 121; *Arthur's Home Magazine,* vol. V, no. 5, May 1855, p. 342; vol. XI, no. 4, April 1858, p. 199.

11. *The Lily,* vol. 6, no. 7, May 1, 1855, p. 67; *The Sibyl,* vol. IV, no. 2, July 15, 1859, pp. 585–586.

12. *Godey's Lady's Book,* vol. XX, no. 1, January 1840, pp. 42–43; no. 2, February 1840, pp. 86–88; no. 4, April 1840, pp. 154–155 and references included in foot-notes 10 and 11.

13. *Godey's Lady's Book,* vol. XX, no. 1, January 1840, pp. 42–43.

14. *Ibid.,* p. 42 quoted by Mrs. Hale.

15. *Ladies' Garland,* vol. VII, new series, vol. I, no. 10, April 1844, pp. 227–228.

16. *Southern Lady's Companion,* vol. II, no. 5, August 1848, p. 17.

17. *Ibid.,* vol. III, no. 4, July 1849, pp. 92–93.

18. *Godey's Lady's Book,* vol. XLVII, no. 1, July 1853, p. 86.

scribed,[19] and editors commented adversely when it was not included in the curriculum. Mrs. Hale concluded a rather long article on the Troy Female Seminary in this way:

Nearly all large seminaries for girls are deficient in this particular; there is no department of household science; but this is soon to be remedied in one denomination, Roman Catholic schools for young ladies. . . . These Catholic schools are popular with many who do not belong to the faith, because of the careful attention paid to the pupils; if this neglected branch of the "science of the *cuisine*" is also taught in those schools the advantage will be increased. We hope "The Vassar College for Young Ladies" will have a department of Health and Household Science; such a department is all that is needed to perfect "The Troy Female Seminary." [20]

Finally, *The Lady's Book,*[21] *Peterson's,*[22] *Miss Leslie's Magazine*[23] vied with each other in giving "receipts." These "receipts" are remarkable for their lack of definiteness either in quantity of materials or in directions for procedure. At times with equal lack of precision, Mrs. Hale chatted with her readers on such topics as "Brown or Dyspepsia Bread"[24] and "Household Vinegars."[25] More specific were directions for crocheting,[26] lace-making,[27] and knitting;[28] but instructions for making a dress by means of a diagram which needed to be doubled to get the size of a pattern and then

19. See Chapter V.
20. *Godey's Lady's Book,* vol. LXI, no. 4, October 1860, p. 369 (entire article pp. 368–369).
21. *Ibid.,* vol. XX, no. 1, January 1840, p. 43; no. 2, February 1840, p. 87, etc.
22. *Ladies' National Magazine,* vol. VII, no. 3, September 1845, p. 107; no. 4, October 1845, p. 143; no. 6, December 1845, p. 178, etc.
23. *Miss Leslie's Magazine,* vol. 1, no. 4, April 1843, pp. 146–147; vol. II, no. 2, August 1843, p. 68; no. 3, September 1843, pp. 102–103; no. 4, October 1843, pp. 138–139; no. 6, December 1843, p. 211.
24. *Godey's Lady's Book,* vol. XX, no. 1, January 1840, p. 43.
25. *Ibid.,* no. 4, April 1840, p. 156.
26. *Ibid.,* vol. LIV, no. 1, January 1857, pp. 40–41; no. 2, February 1857, pp. 136–138.
27. *Peterson's Ladies' National Magazine,* vol. XXXI, no. 4, April, 1857, p. 313.
28. *Ibid.,* vol. XXXVII, no. 1, January 1860, p. 85.

adjusted to fit the individual [29] must have sent the gentle reader for a seamstress.

The whole subject of domestic economy as seen in the ladies' magazines of the decades before the Civil War whether in editorial discussions or as a project in adult education, has the characteristic of the testimonial. In the same spirit were women and girls urged to learn to use the newly developed sewing machine,[30] and Dr. E. Thompson took "his pen in hand" to show that if young ladies were taught Chemistry they would "thereby be better qualified to super-intend domestic affairs, guard against many accidents to which households are subject, and perhaps be instrumental in saving life." [31]

With even greater ardor writers in the ladies' magazines endorsed physical education for girls. They discussed its value as a subject in the curriculum.[32] The keynote of most of their articles was the need for a sound body to house a sound mind.[33] The development of the body should keep pace with that of the mind.[34] A Scotch physician was quoted to show that until a girl was fourteen or fifteen she should be allowed to play at least six hours of every day in the open air.[35] A comparison between English and American girls indicated the need for more physical education in America.[36] It was believed that physical education would help make girls and women stronger and consequently better wives and mothers.[37]

29. *Ibid.,* vol. XXXI, no. 2, February 1857, pp. 159–160.

30. *The Lily,* vol. 1, no. 9, October 1, 1849, p. 80; *Godey's Lady's Book,* vol. LX, no. 4, April 1860, pp. 369–370.

31. *Ladies' Garland,* vol. IV, (part I) no. 1, January 1850, pp. 25–26.

32. *Godey's Lady's Book,* vol. LII, no. 2, February 1856, pp. 178–179, quoted at length from an article in *Southern Quarterly Review,* vol. XXVII (new series vol. XI) April 1855, pp. 451–475; *Godey's Lady's Book,* vol. LIV, no. 3, March 1857, p. 275; *Ladies' Garland,* vol. VII, new series, vol. I, no. 10, April 1844, pp. 227–228 (article by Catharine Beecher).

33. *Godey's Lady's Book,* vol. LIV, no. 3, March 1857, p. 275; *Home Journal,* whole no. 326, series for 1852, no. 19, May 6, 1852, p. 129; *Ladies' Companion,* vol. 7, no. 1, January 1837, p. 19; *The Sibyl,* vol. II, no. 10, November 15, 1857, p. 270.

34. *Arthur's Home Magazine,* vol. XIII, no. 6, June 1859, pp. 284–285.

35. *Godey's Lady's Book,* vol. XXIII, no. 3, September 1841, p. 119.

36. *Southern Lady's Companion,* vol. V, no. 4, July 1851, p. 101.

37. *Peterson's Ladies' National Magazine,* vol. XXII, no. 5, November 1852, pp. 232–235.

To several writers physical education meant not a subject to be pursued but healthful living.[38] They presented their point of view in a number of ways. "The Boarding School Nuisance" was attacked by a physician.

. . . The pupils rise at five in the morning. They study from five to seven o'clock. From seven to eight they have breakfast. From eight in the morning to two P. M. is spent in the school room, a period of six hours. At two they have dinner; and from three to five they are allowed to walk or take other exercise. From five to six they study; at six have tea, and then study from seven to nine, when they are sent to bed.

Their diet is light and unsubstantial, and their appetites under such a regimen are feeble as the diet.

Now, here the day of a young, growing, spirited school girl is divided into periods of seven hours for sleep, three for meals, two for exercise, and twelve for study. Every person under full adult age needs eight or nine hours sleep; and in order that the sleep should be healthful and refreshing, they require at least six hours of recreation and active exercise. The time for meals is sufficiently ample in the instance here mentioned, but to allow only two hours for exercise and that in the afternoon, when heat and fatigue dispose them to rest, is positively murderous. And twelve hours study per day is at least five hours too much for any young person. . . .[39]

Nor was the cry of too much work in school raised only against the boarding schools for girls. In the Editor's Department of *Arthur's Home Magazine* appeared a similar indictment of the public schools.

Too Many Hours in School and Too Many Lessons out of School

Our public schools are fast destroying the health of our children by overtaxing their minds and their bodies. Five, six and seven hours' confinement in school during the day, is of itself sufficient to impair the health even of a robust child; but when close mental application during those hours, and two or three hours of study out of school are

38. *The Presbyterian Casket of Sacred and Polite Literature,* vol. I, no. II, January 1851, pp. 48–49 ("Fashionable Education" by George Moore, M.D.); *Frontier Monthly,* vol. I, no. 2, May 1859, pp. 70–72 (Editor's Table).

39. Quoted from the *Buffalo Medical Journal* in *Frank Leslie's Illustrated Newspaper,* vol. I, no. 18, April 12, 1856, p. 285.

added, the wonder is the shamefully wronged little ones bear up
as well as they do. No labor is so exhausting as that of the mind. . . .[40]

A writer in the *Physio Medical Recorder* felt that girls should be
encouraged "to ride, run, walk, dance in the open air" and "to plant
and cultivate a garden." [41] After recommending bathing as a health
habit, the practical Mrs. Swisshelm suggested that communities erect
bathing houses at the water's edge.[42] Miss Beecher, to, advocated
a daily bath.[43]

Calisthenics,[44] swimming, equestrianism and dancing were commended to the readers of the magazines. Descriptions of swimming
and swimming exhibitions were given,[45] and Mrs. Hale in her "Aids
in Learning to Swim" gave a graphic picture of what she considered
desirable.

. . . Probably one of the best ways of learning to swim is to go with
a competent teacher, in a boat to deep water, this supporting the
body more buoyantly than that which is shallower, and preventing
the constant tendency of beginners to touch the bottom, which is here
of course impossible.

The teacher should fasten a rope carefully around the waist, or
better still to a belt, which can neither tighten or slip down. The
rope may be fastened to a short pole. Supported in this manner,
the pupil may take his proper position in the water, and practice
the necessary motions, and the support of the rope may be gradually
lessened, until the pupil finds himself entirely supported by water. . . .[46]

Discussions of equestrianism involved matters of dress and etiquette
as well as horsemanship.[47] Although it was not so stated, riding and

40. *Arthur's Home Magazine,* vol. V, no. 5, May 1855, p. 339.
41. Quoted in *The Sibyl,* vol. II, no. 5, September 1, 1857, p. 230.
42. *Pittsburgh Saturday Visiter,* vol. II, no. 30, August 11, 1849, p. 118.
43. *Ladies' Repository,* vol. XIII, no. 1, January 1853, p. 28.
44. *Godey's Lady's Book,* vol. XXXVII, no. 2, August 1848, pp. 111–112.
45. *Godey's Lady's Book,* vol. LVII, no. 5, November 1858, pp. 466–468;
vol. LX, no. 4, April 1860, pp. 369–370; no. 6, June 1860, pp. 493–497; *Ladies'
Companion,* vol. 7, no. 1, May 1837, pp. 39–40; *The Sibyl,* vol. IV, no. XIII,
January 1, 1860, p. 678.
46. *Godey's Lady's Book,* vol. LVII, no. 2, August 1858, pp. 123–124
(entire article, pp. 123–125).
47. *Ibid.,* vol. XLIII, no. 1, July 1851, pp. 27–29; *Peterson's Ladies' Na-*

frequently dancing were treated in the ladies' magazines as "accomplishments." Mrs. Hale, however, in discussing the dance stressed the value of "the measured movements" which gave "grace and strength to the limbs" and of the "appropriate social amusement for young people" which encouraged "life and gayety; while it checked romping." [48] Methodist writers condemned dancing as a peril to the salvation of the soul.[49]

While dancing did not meet with approval of all the writers physical education for girls and boys was usually endorsed. About 1790 Dr. Benjamin Rush had recommended that intellectual and physical training receive attention together; two German refugees, Charles Beck and Charles Follen, helped to promote an interest in it in the 1820's; but it was not until the late 1850's that the efforts of the champions of physical education began to bear fruit and girls benefited as well as boys.[50] Only "accomplishments" and domestic economy were looked upon as the prerogative of women and girls. Consequently other curricula for girls must be seen against the background of the curricula for boys.

Until the end of the first quarter of the nineteenth century, local school districts determined the policy of the elementary schools. While these schools were public, they were often not free.[51] Even in New England girls sometimes attended only during the summer, when boys were at work.[52] In addition to the public schools, there

tional Magazine, vol. XV, no. 3, March 1849, pp. 112–113; no. 5, May 1849, pp. 184–185; vol. XVI, no. 1, July 1849, p. 44; no. 2, August 1849, p. 84; no. 5, November 1849, p. 187; vol. XXI, January 1852, p. 81; no. 2, February 1852, p. 129; no. 3, March 1852, p. 170; no. 4, April 1852, p. 229; no. 5, May 1852, p. 269; no. 6, June 1852, p. 305; vol. XXII, no. 1, July 1852, p. 69; no. 2, August 1852, p. 100; no. 3, September 1852, p. 149; no. 4, October 1852, p. 189; *Miss Leslie's Magazine,* vol. 2, no. 5, November 1843, pp. 156–158.

48. *Godey's Lady's Book,* vol. LV, no. 4, October 1857, pp. 369–370. Similar ideas were expressed in *American Ladies' Magazine,* vol. VI, no. 12, December 1833, pp. 539–545.

49. *Southern Lady's Companion,* vol. V, no. 6, September 1851, pp. 174–175; *Ladies' Repository,* vol. XIV, no. 4, April 1854, pp. 145–149; no. 5, May 1854, pp. 224–227.

50. Noble, *op. cit.,* pp. 242, 243.

51. Edward H. Reisner, *The Evolution of the Common School* (New York, The Macmillan Company, 1935, pp. x, 590), pp 307 ff.

52. *The Sibyl,* vol. IV, no. IV, August 15, 1859, p. 607.

were private schools, often connected with churches. In both kinds of elementary schools, learning seems to have been confined to the three R's. To give more education to boys, academies were established and flourished until the Civil War; high schools came into existence in the second quarter of the nineteenth century.[53] Secondary schools like colleges gave a general education, a curriculum of culture. It was this curriculum of culture to which the crusading women aspired and which discriminating men, who recognized woman's right to an education, or desired a wife to be a companion, endorsed.

What was this curriculum of culture? The classics, especially Latin, English grammar, rhetoric and composition, literature, civil government and history, modern languages, mathematics, including advanced arithmetic, algebra and geometry, the sciences, such as natural philosophy, geography, botany and physiology, drawing and singing, and one vocational subject, book-keeping.[54] For the most part the subjects which were advocated in the ladies' magazines were the subjects which were relatively new in the curriculum. To some there was no need to champion the classics with their centuries of educational tradition. Mrs. Hale, however, in discussing the Baltimore Young Ladies' College at Baltimore City, stated ". . . The only point in it which does not strike us favorably is the time devoted to the dead languages; while those spoken now and in which the present work of the world must be performed, are comparatively neglected. English composition, however, receives the attention it merits, and is placed as it should be in the first rank. . . ." [55] Generally a discussion of whether girls should be taught Latin involved their mental ability, not the value of Latin.

The German magazines stressed the value of teaching German and of having German children attend German schools in order that German culture be preserved.[56]

In connection with domestic economy, chemistry [57] and book-

53. Reisner, *op. cit.*, pp. 314–316.   54. Noble, *op. cit.*, pp. 219–245.
55. *Godey's Lady's Book*, vol. LVIII, no. 1, January 1859, p. 81.
56. *Atlantis*, Neu Folge, Band 3, Heft 2, August 1855, pp. 175–178; *Didaskalia*, Zweites Heft, pp. 290–296; *Frank Leslie's Illustrirte Zeitung*, Band VI, no. 1, 18 Februar, 1860, p. 14.
57. *Ladies' Garland*, vol. IV (part I), no. 1, January 1850, pp. 25–26.

keeping [58] were endorsed. The alliance between chemistry and physiology was noted.[59] Glowing tributes were paid to the study of history.[60] Elizabeth Palmer Peabody stated well the value of the study of history.

. . . And I think that history is the proper study to unfold the intellect of woman, into all those exercises which shall fit her for those duties. As Emerson has said, we can judge our own characteristics, and those of others when they are displayed on the page of history, without personal pique. The same passions that play around us in our neighborhood, have determined national events. There is in our own circle of acquaintances, the ancient Greek and Roman, and every other nationality; and here too, we may see the Washingtons and Benedict Arnolds, the Julius Caesar and Caesar Borgia *in little*. To learn by inference from the phenomenon of these miniatures, the moral results of their characteristics, and the relation of their various activities to the Eternal Laws, would take our whole life time; and we need their knowledge with which to begin our life-work. But God has already pronounced judgment on all these characteristics; and it is recorded by the iron finger of time on the page of history. . . . It is the most important of studies for all republicans. It is not necessary for every man to be an astronomer, chemist, linguist; but it is inevitable for every man to be a citizen, and of a country which every voter contributes to govern, of a country whose future is affected by every vote. History has always been taught to those who are expected to manage states; and every American has in some degree the function of a statesman, and should have something of a statesman's education. It is the first time in the ages, when the mass of people have had a voice in public affairs, and therefore the first time when it has been obviously necessary that the mass of people should know those universal principles of policy that may peril or preserve the liberty and welfare of a nation within itself and with relation to other nations. . . .[61]

58. *Southern Lady's Companion,* vol. III, no. 4, July 1849, pp. 92–93.
59. *The Western Journal of Agriculture, Manufacture, Mechanic Arts, Internal Improvement, Commerce and General Literature,* vol. VI, no. 1, April 1851, pp. 94–103.
60. *The Una,* vol. III, no. 2, February 1855, pp. 28–29; vol. III, no. 3, March 1855, pp. 37–38; no. IV, April 1855, pp. 50–51; *The Atlantic Monthly,* vol. VI, no. 35, September 1860, pp. 298–309.
61. *The Una,* vol. III, no. 2, February 1855, pp. 28–29.

Comments on other subjects were sporadic. The importance of speaking good English was stressed; parents were urged to train their children in the habits of correct speech.[62] The desirability of cultivating among young people a love of good books [63] and a taste for literature [64] was indicated. It was recommended that parents give special attention to the kinds of newspapers children read.[65] Music was looked upon as a great moral force; it could make the sabbath a delight,[66] but unfortunately it was being "perverted" in the "trashy and effeminate secular music of the time" as it had been in war music.[67] Parents were urged to allow their children to learn to play a musical instrument. Ten was not too early for children to begin and "if it [was] possible, they should not be allowed to practice alone for a year at least, as "bad habits [were] formed." [68]

Writers who were interested in cultivating woman's influence felt girls should learn "to perceive the beautiful" [69] and that they should be qualified to teach children useful lessons in almost every department of knowledge.[70] They could more easily describe the ideal woman than select subjects for her instruction. At times it seems as if they felt the power of influencing which they coveted for her could not be taught, but that it might be caught. Most of all they wanted woman to influence the character of husband and children, but they knew not how to teach her this art.

Despite the fact that practically all the aims of education that found expression in the popular magazines either directly stated or

62. *Southern Lady's Companion,* vol. II, no. 11, February 1, 1849, pp. 241–242.

63. *The Lily,* vol. I, no. 1, January 1, 1849, p. 3; *The Western Journal of Agriculture, Manufacture, Mechanic Arts, Internal Improvement, Commerce and General Literature,* vol. V, no. IV, January 1851, pp. 206–208 ("Female Education" by Mrs. Harriet Westbrook).

64. *The Universalist and Ladies' Repository,* vol. 9, no. 4, September 1840, p. 158.

65. *Southern Lady's Companion,* vol. 5, no. 10, January 1852, p. 308.

66. *Advocate of Moral Reform,* vol. VII, no. 5, March 1, 1841, pp. 36–37.

67. *Ladies' Garland,* vol. IV (part I), no. 4, April 1850, pp. 104–106.

68. *Godey's Lady's Book,* vol. XLV, no. 4, October 1852, p. 396.

69. *Godey's Lady's Book,* vol. XX, no. 1, January 1840, pp. 9–11. "The Perception of the Beautiful" by Mrs. L. H. Sigourney.

70. *Ladies' Repository,* vol. XIII, no. 8, August 1853, pp. 366–368.

implied the desirability of the development of high ethical character,[71] those same magazines practically ignored religious and ethical training. They would teach a girl divinity and have her read the Bible. The payment of pew rent implied attendance at Church. But definite religious instruction was omitted from the curriculum.

This situation may have come from a number of reasons. To most Protestants, and most of the editors were members of the various Protestant denominations, Bible reading and interpretation of the Bible in church and sunday school constituted the way to teach religion. Moreover, each denomination had its own set of dogmas, and it is quite possible the editors of secular literature, who needed the support of subscribers, were unwilling to be drawn into any theological controversy. On the other hand, the lack of direct religious and ethical instruction may have been a reflection of the American individualization of religion. Freedom of worship was protected by the first amendment to the Constitution. By 1821 Church and government had been separated in all the states. Furthermore throughout the pre-Civil War decades, most of the states in their school legislation indicated that there should be no religious instruction in the public schools. A fourth possible explanation might lie in the belief that character is best taught by example. Many illustrations of ways in which a mother could influence her children through example appeared in the ladies' magazines.[72] The writers probably believed that any teacher would utilize every opportunity to correct faults in the character of his pupils. Be that as it may, religion and ethics were not included in the curricula for young ladies as presented in the pages of the popular periodicals.

These magazines reflected the thinking of the educational leaders of the period. The two subjects most often endorsed—home economics and physical education—had the ardent support of a goodly number of educators. Leaders in opening educational opportunities for girls never forgot that most of the girls would become wives and mothers and would, therefore, need to know domestic economy. Educators recommended physical education for boys and girls. They deemed a cultural curriculum desirable for both sexes. By 1860 there

71. See Chapter II.　　　　72. See Chapter VIII.

were many schools where a girl could pursue such a curriculum of culture. In fact, the preceding decades marked a steady growth both in schools for girls and opportunities within schools. Only parents, practical head-mistresses, and realistic editors recognized the value of "accomplishments" for an "educated" young lady.

CHAPTER FIVE

Educational Opportunities under Private Auspices

*A*s the leaders in education for women modeled the curriculum for girls on the accepted one for boys, so they often imitated boys' schools in the schools for girls. There were two kinds of schools for boys where subjects more advanced than the three R's were taught. The first of these historically was the Latin Grammar School. This type of school was prevalent in all the colonies except Georgia and was patterned on the Latin Grammar School of England, which had grown from the influence of the Renaissance and Reformation. Because it was a socially exclusive school, to which the students paid tuition, and an academically exclusive one, where the work was confined almost entirely to Latin and Greek, it was never popular. Few Latin Grammar Schools survived to the nineteenth century. Their place was taken by the Academy. Academies began about the middle of the eighteenth century, flourished in all parts of the country and reached the period of their greatest expansion in the first half of the nineteenth century. They were not so socially exclusive as the Grammar Schools, for, while they charged tuition, they often taught poor children free, in exchange for special privileges granted by the state. They were not so academically exclusive in that they added to the curriculum mathematics before 1800, geography about 1807, English grammar about 1819, and subsequently other subjects, such as algebra, geometry, American history, ancient history, belles-lettres, rhetoric, ethics, metaphysics, and trigonometry.

As suggested by the growing curriculum, education for boys was undergoing many changes. These changes were along three lines,—

changes in subject matter and method, changes in student personnel, and changes in the financing of schools. The last two changes were interdependent. As the government (city, county, state) assumed responsibility for the financing of elementary and secondary schools, education was made available to the children of all the people. In 1821 the first public high school was established in Boston. The public high school was a peculiarly American institution and had roots in both the common school and the academy.[1]

Academies varied greatly. There were those for boys alone, for girls alone, for boys and girls together. Some were endowed; others were owned by individuals; still others were chartered by state legislatures; and a few even received state aid. Several included elementary subjects in the curriculum, even for their adolescent students; most of them were secondary schools; a few reached the college level. Some translated the ideas of Rousseau, Pestalozzi and other European educators into an American model.[2]

The magazines for ladies and gentlemen mirrored the heterogeneous character of the academies, and editors took definite leadership in educational battles, particularly those of the 1850's. No question was more discussed than that of coeducation.

The battle for coeducation was fought with logic and enthusiasm. To the editorial minds, there was just one side to the question. Coeducation was "the proper way. God places the children of both sexes in the same family, together they attend divine worship, why should not both sexes be together in places of education?" It was a question that was reiterated and always answered in the affirmative by the very editors who gave lengthy descriptions and enthusiastic commendation to schools for girls. They marshalled the arguments for coeducation. It was God's way. It was convenient for parents to send their children to the same school. It developed good manners and morals.[3] Mrs. Stow, a celebrated teacher of Glasgow, was quoted to show the advantages of coeducation in developing a higher moral standard among the Scotch than was brought about in France by the

1. See chapter VI, "Public Education."
2. Knight, *op. cit.*, pp. 112–114; 373–386; Eby and Arrowood, *The Development of Modern Education* (New York, Prentice Hall, inc., xxiv, 922 pp.) pp. 725–726, 748–751; Woody, *op. cit.*, vol. I, chs. 8 and 9.
3. *Godey's Lady's Book,* vol. LII, no. 4, April 1856, p. 372.

separate education of the sexes.[4] The editors of *The Lily*,[5] *The Una* [6] and *The Sibyl* [7] championed the cause of coeducation. Mrs. Swisshelm from her experience as a pupil and a teacher wrote a persuasive editorial in her *Pittsburgh Saturday Visiter*.

Dear gentle reader, do you belong to the good old days when all the children in the family went to the same school? . . . If you do you can sympathize with us in our dislike of this modern improvement of separating the sexes. Cannot say that it is very modern either! It has existed ever since there was a nunnery; and those who believe in nunneries—believe that the highest state of perfection here requires celibacy, are consistent in the matter! If being educated is being prepared for the duties of life, one would suppose that the rising generation were to be monks and nuns! . . . Put these young people into the same institution—the same classes, under the care of the same teachers and you make rivals, friends, almost anything but lovers of them. You give a stimulus to study which can be given in no other way. . . . They get a more just and rational knowledge of each other; and if any intimacy commences that ends in marriage, it will be much more likely to be a happy one than if the acquaintance had begun and terminated in the present fashionable mode. . . . No amount of vigilance of teachers can compensate for the restraint one sex has upon the other! No artificial stimulant can equal the generous rivalry that exists in a class where they stand side by side. There will be more study—more friendship—more every-day common sense and less billet doux writing—less love, less sentimentality, than if they were at different ends of the house and square. . . .[8]

It was cause for gratification that the New York Central College,[9] Oberlin [10] and Antioch [11] admitted women as well as men. Mrs. Davis,

4. *Ibid.*, vol. LI, no. 1, July 1855, p. 372; and *Arthur's Home Magazine*, vol. XI, no. 1, January 1858, p. 27.

5. Reply to Mrs. Bloomer and Mrs. Davis in *Pittsburgh Saturday Visiter*, vol. IV, no. 7, March 8, 1851, p. 26.

6. *The Una*, vol. I, no. 8, August 20, 1853, p. 121 and vol. II, no. 11, November 1854, p. 361.

7. *The Sibyl*, vol. I, no. 5, September 1, 1856, p. 37.

8. *Pittsburgh Saturday Visiter*, vol. II, no. 13, April 14, 1849, p. 50.

9. *The Una*, vol. II, no. 11, November 1854, p. 361 and *The Sibyl*, vol. I, no. 5, September 1, 1856, p. 37.

10. *The Una*, vol. II, no. 11, November 1854, p. 361 and *Godey's Lady's Book*, vol. LIII, no. 4, October 1856, p. 372.

in *The Una,* noted that the faculty of Antioch included "Miss R. M.
Pennell, Professor of Physical Geography, Drawing, Natural History and Dialectic"; she hoped that two of the unfilled professors'
chairs would be occupied by women and concluded by saying "This
college starts on the right ground and we gladly bid it God speed." [12]
Mrs. Hale wished that "Mound Prairie Institute . . . a new seminary for both sexes lately opened at Mound Prairie, Anderson
County, Texas" would be "well patronized and prosper largely." [13]
Despite the championship of the women editors and many leaders
in education, coeducational secondary schools seem to have constituted a very small minority. The few described in the magazines,
usually possessed other unusual features. Such a progressive institution was the Raritan Bay Union School, which was organized as
a family school and was located a mile from the steamboat landing
at Perth Amboy, New Jersey. Accommodations were provided for
forty or fifty boarding pupils, who with a few children of resident
members, constituted the student body. A vegetarian table was provided and neither coffee nor tea was used, because they believed
both to be "injurious to children and youth." There were two ses-
sions of twenty weeks each, with a three weeks vacation at Christmas,
a week in April and a long vacation from "the latter part of July
to the end of September." The school opened October 1, 1854. The
cost was a hundred dollars for each session, which defrayed "the
expense of board, washing, to the extent of one dozen pieces per
week, bed, bedding, rooms and room furniture, fuel, lights, tuition,
use of apparatus, library, gymnasium, etc." However, if pupils
studied in their rooms, fuel and light were charged extra and there
was a charge for "instruction on the piano and use of the instrument." Each pupil was required to provide himself with "four towels,
four table napkins, and two pairs of slippers" and to mark each
piece of clothing with his full name.

The faculty was outstanding. The "special teachers" were: Theodore D. Weld, Elizabeth P. Peabody, Margaret Corliss, Ann Eliza

11. *The Una,* vol. I, no. 8, August 20, 1853, p. 121 and *Godey's Lady's
Book,* vol. LIII, no. 4, October 1856, p. 372.
12. *The Una,* vol. I, no. 8, August 20, 1853, p. 121.
13. *Godey's Lady's Book,* vol. LII, no. 4, April 1856, p. 372.

Youmans; and the "occasional teachers" were: William H. Channing, Edward L. Youmans, Angelina G. Weld, Sarah M. Grimké. The curriculum included "the sciences of Nature, Intellectual and Material, History, the usual Ancient and Modern Languages; drawing, according to the principles of Art and Descriptive Geometry, and Vocal and Instrumental Music," Agriculture, Horticulture, and Mechanical Arts. Provision was made for teaching in accordance with "the capacity of the scholar," so that "no artificial stimulus" of emulation would be needed. In these ways and in the use of observation, practice and development of manual skills,[14] they followed the ideas of Pestalozzi and Fellenberg.

The Albany Manual Labor College of Albany, Athens County, Ohio, also proposed to combine manual labor and study in order "to rebuke the withering spirit of *caste*, . . . make all forms of useful industry respectable, and furnish the community with *practical* men and women instead of mere theorists. . . ."[15] Thus education could be a great democratizing force.

In Worcester, Massachusetts, were two interesting coeducational institutions, the School of Design and the French Institute. These were closely connected. At the School of Design, which was "not as its name would seem to indicate an institution devoted to a single purpose, but a place where a thorough and liberal education could be acquired," children "of the earliest ages" and of both sexes were "instructed in the rudiments of English, French, Music and drawing at the same time, so that all faculties of the mind are harmoniously developed." [16]

The French Institute stressed training in languages.

The object of the French Institute is to give a complete academical [sic] education to youth of both sexes; the different branches of study to be pursued in English and French, under native teachers, affording a rare opportunity to acquire familiarity with the French language, *as spoken in Paris*. Facilities are here enjoyed for a complete education, be it classical, scientific, literary or artistic. French and German are constantly spoken in the family of the principals.

14. *The Una,* vol. II, no. 8, August 1854, p. 311.
15. *Pittsburgh Saturday Visiter,* vol. II, no. 14, April 21, 1849, p. 55.
16. *Godey's Lady's Book,* vol. LVIII, no. 2, February 1859, pp. 176–177.

The school embraces students of all ages, from the child taking its first step in knowledge, to the youth who is preparing for college. The system pursued makes the study a pleasure rather than a task, pupils receiving encouragement and assistance from teachers. . . . [Singing, calesthenics and military drill are provided.] . . . Discipline is firm without being severe. In this way they learn to accomplish much that is generally considered beyond the reach of children, and lay, in addition, a solid basis for the acquisition of knowledge in after years. Their tastes are guided in the right direction and a love of all that is beautiful in nature and in art is inculcated. To this end the school rooms are pleasant parlors, hung with the best engravings and ornamented with the choicest flowers. Children are easily impressed by surrounding influences, and with those to whom their education is intrusted rests the responsibility of inculcating tastes that shall purify and bless their lives,—tastes which the majority of children do not acquire without aid.

Feeling a deep interest in the education of youth of both sexes, we have looked upon this school as, in every respect, a *model institution*. We are aware that this is high praise; but those acquainted with its merits will respond in all sincerity. . . .[17]

The French Institute was one of the few schools where German as well as French was spoken. German schools were, however, advocated in German magazines. Courses of study were given in detail and parents were urged to send their children that German culture might be preserved.[18]

Mrs. Davis found satisfaction in the wider interests of a progressive school for girls, the Sharon Boarding School, near Chester, Pennsylvania, where there were about "forty bright young girls, full of intelligence and newly awakened thought." There, too, were put into practice ideas of European philosophers and educators. The aim of John and Rachel Jackson was to set their pupils to

17. *Ibid.*, vol. LIX, no. 3, September 1859, p. 274.
18. *Atlantis*, neue Folge, Band 3, Heft 4, Oktober 1855, pp. 279–284; Blätter für Freies Religiöses Leben, 4ter Jahrgang, no. 6, December 1859, pp. 92–95; no. 12, June 1860, p. 192; Das Brüder-Blatt, 1ster Jahrgang, no. 7, July 1854, pp. 165–167; *Didaskalia*, Zweites Heft, pp. 290–296; *Frank Leslie's Illustrirte Zeitung*, Band VI, no. 1, 18 Februar, 1860, p. 14.

thinking and reasoning, to cultivate the heart and to make them true and noble women.

To accomplish this they throw the pupil upon her own resources. She is not governed, watched and perpetually tutored, but is taught that she must govern herself; must watch over her own untoward propensities and learn to control them; is made to feel that she is a responsible being. Under this system of training the youngest child soon comes to feel that to do right when alone is a greater pleasure than to cheat and deceive. Hence in warm agreeable weather, the garden, the orchard, the woods and lawn are equally the school room, and the beneficial effects of this freedom is seen in their clear healthy complexions and well developed physiques. The studies are thorough and systematic, the means and appliances for illustration are superior to almost, perhaps we may say, any other boarding school. Connected with the school room is a fine laboratory where the lessons in Chemistry are illustrated by experiments. They have a large and excellent telescope worth $2,000 with a sidereal clock, and various astronomical instruments which are used by the pupils. A life size French manakin and a large number of exceedingly fine anatomical plates are provided for the study of physiology. We also observed large historical charts and maps, a beautiful microscope, etc. In addition to these facilities for teaching they often invite popular lecturers on various sciences to visit the school. This excellent training does not appear to us calculated to raise up a class of discontented shallow philosophers, still we could not but ask whether these girls who feel themselves responsible beings there, will not when they come out into the active world, desire to govern themselves, and to still feel they have an individual life, for which they are accountable to the highest. . . .[19]

A few women recognized that the garden and the orchard might provide vocational as well as general training and a School of Horticulture for Orphaned Girls was established on Long Island.[20] Michigan founded an agricultural college, but women were unsuccessful in gaining admission.[21]

19. *The Una*, vol. II, no. 6, June 1854, p. 286. Described also in *Pennsylvania School Journal*, vol. I, no. 8, August 1852, pp. 130–131.
20. *The Sibyl*, vol. III, no. 24, June 15, 1859, p. 570.
21. *Ibid.*, vol. II, no. 7, October 1, 1857, p. 242.

Sometimes the women editors departed from the role of chronicler of educational experiments to plead for funds to support these experiments. Mrs. Davis performed such a service for the New England School of Design for Women. She gave a history of the school but the crux of her argument centered about the need for such an institution.

. . . There is need of educated and professional talent in many of the trades which require the use of ornament in their productions. A higher standard is looked for in all kinds of manufactured goods. The public taste advances with the age, and demands constant progress in the production of all articles whether for use or ornament. It is this want which the School of Design is calculated to supply, and as the result of such application of labor becomes apparent in the increase demand of articles in which taste and utility are combined, the whole community is interested to advance this important object.

The great and leading object of the School is to teach the art of ornamental design and its application to manufacture in all its branches,—the promotion of improvement in the extended application of ornamental art, and the education of a class capable of competing successfully with foreign artists. It is subservient to a great variety of occupations and trades,—to the textile and printed fabrics, carpets, paper hangings, furniture, pottery, porcelain, engraving, sculpture, printing, embroidery and glass,—the silversmith and the jeweler, the worker in iron, brass and other metals,—in short there is hardly any mechanical or manufacturing employment that does not at times require the aid of the skillful designer. . . .[22]

The school was incorporated July 13, 1853 and by the end of that year was reported to thrive.[23] Later, Mrs. Hale rejoiced that "the Women's School of Design in the Peter Cooper Institution of New York City is in a flourishing condition, at least so far as good attendance of pupils goes. There are one hundred thirty-nine who regularly attend their studies, some of them practicing at wood engraving, some at drawing from models, some at oil painting and others at water colors." [24] The first school of this kind in America,

22. *The Una,* vol. I, no. 9, September 1853, pp. 140–141.
23. *Ibid.,* vol. I, no. 12, December 1853, pp. 156–157.
24. *Godey's Lady's Book,* vol. LX, no. 5, May 1860, p. 468.

however, was the Philadelphia School of Design for Women, founded in 1848 by Mrs. Sarah Peter. Subsequently, it was incorporated "with a Board of gentlemen Managers, from among the most eminent citizens of Philadelphia and a Board of lady Assistant Managers, who attended to the internal affairs of the school, the admission of pupils, their deportment, proficiency, etc." By 1854 "an endowment of $50,000" was "in hopeful progress." [25]

Despite the editorial interest in unusual educational opportunities, the good private school, where young ladies were properly educated for their "sphere," was the customary school for girls. Such institutions met with the kindly interest of the editor of *Godey's Lady's Book* and received from her a great deal of free advertising. She frequently called the attention of her readers to Miss S. J. Hale's Boarding and Day School for Young Ladies. The house it occupied at 922 Spruce Street, Philadelphia, is still standing,—a four story brick dwelling, with the distinctive portico that caused the row of houses to be called "Portico Square." [26] The school combined "in an unusual degree the comforts of home with the discipline and regularity of a school. The health and deportment as well as the intellectual advancement of the scholars [had] attention. The course of English study was thorough and liberal. A superior French teacher resid[ed] in the family to aid in conversation." Music, dancing and other accomplishments were well taught.[27] A home-like atmosphere, where it was hoped girls would absorb the qualities of a well-bred woman, and a resident French teacher, usually a native French woman, were characteristics of many private secondary schools for girls. Education was not considered simply book learning; it included "the guiding and developing of the human heart, the taste and ruling passion" in order to fit a young lady for her future life, whether in town or country, among the well-to-do or people of modest means.

A mother should be wise in selecting a school for her daughter. Mrs. Hale gave pointed advice:

25. *Ibid.*, vol. XLVIII, no. 3, March 1854, p. 271.
26. *Ibid.*, vol. LVI, April 1858, p. 373.
27. *Ibid.*, vol. LVIII, no. 1, January 1859, p. 81.

If a Northern woman expected to spend her days in the atmosphere
of Boston, were sent to study in the extreme South, surrounded by
entirely different customs and habits from those which she would
find at home, we should not think it *judicious,* at least, to spend three
years in forming associations she would soon be required to resign
altogether. So of the South sending to us; in many instances, the
style of living being so entirely dissimilar, the very housekeeping
being a separate study by itself, and the household associations more
peculiar than that of any country one could name. The love of home
and home surroundings should be fostered, not checked, or a real
wrong is done to the absent child expected to return home perma-
nently to its shelter. . . .[28]

Thereupon, she recommended two Southern schools, the Charleston
School, conducted by the Misses Bates, and the Yalobusha Baptist
Female Institute of Granada, Mississippi. There were many fa-
vorable comments upon the Patapsco Female Seminary, founded in
1841, near Baltimore, by Mrs. Lincoln Phelps, sister of Mrs. Emma
Willard.[29] In recommending the Lynchburg Young Ladies' Seminary, Mrs. Hale noted that "Virginia is awakening to the importance
of educating her daughters at home." [30] She was not the only editor to
recommend Southern schools for Southern girls. Writers in *The
Southern Literary Messenger,*[31] the *Southern Quarterly Review,*[32]
DeBow's Review [33] gave similar advice but for a very different
reason. To the writers in the Southern periodicals it was necessary
that Southern institutions be preserved and they looked upon education as a means to that end. Consequently they wished "home education" for both boys and girls. To Mrs. Hale it was important that

28. *Ibid.,* vol. XLVI, no. 3, March 1853, p. 285.
29. *Ibid.,* vol. XXIV, no. 4, April 1842, p. 240; vol. XLIX, no. 5, November 1854, pp. 460–461; vol. LI, December 1855, p. 559; vol. LII, no. 5, May
1856, p. 467; no. 6, June 1856, p. 560.
30. *Ibid.,* vol. LIV, no. 2, February 1857, pp. 179–180.
31. *Southern Literary Messenger,* vol. XVIII, no. 2, February 1852, pp.
116–122.
32. *Southern Quarterly Review,* vol. II, no. 4, October 1842, p. 421 (comment on boys leaving the South to study); vol. XXI, no. 42, new series,
vol. V, no. X, April 1852, pp. 507–535 (text books).
33. *DeBow's Review of Southern and Western States,* vol. X o.s., second
series vol. IV, third series vol. II, no. 3, March 1851, pp. 362–363.

girls should be suitably prepared to occupy their "sphere," so that they would be well-adjusted, happy women.

In this spirit, Mrs. Hale recommended Western schools, as Mt. Carroll Seminary, a school for "young ladies and gentlemen" at Carroll County, Illinois; [34] New England schools, as New Ipswich Appleton Academy at New Ipswich, New Hampshire, [35] and Mystic Hall, a seminary for young ladies on the Mystic River, near Boston; [36] New York schools, as the Ontario Young Ladies' Seminary at Canandaigua, [37] the Albany Female Academy, the oldest of its kind in the United States, founded in 1814, [38] and the North Granville Female Seminary; [39] country schools, as the Oxford Ladies' Seminary at Oxford, Chester County, Pennsylvania; [40] city schools, as Miss Comegy's Family and Boarding School for Young Ladies, no. 15 East 31 Street, New York City and a Young Ladies' Seminary at 254 Walnut Street, Philadelphia. [41] Religious affiliation rather than locality might be the basis of selection. Mrs. Hale suggested the Moravian School at Bethlehem, Pennsylvania, [42] Episcopal schools as St. Mary's at Burlington, New Jersey [43] and Mrs. Phelps School at Patapsco, [44] Catholic schools [45] and Methodist Colleges. [46] The editor of the *Lady's Book* constantly endeavored to present her readers with a variety of good secondary schools for girls.

Seminaries were sometimes known as "colleges." Yet "college" often seems to have been a courtesy title, as in the case of the Bourbon Collegiate Institute, directed by the Reverend Dr. Mitchell and

34. *Godey's Lady's Book,* vol. LXI, December 1860, p. 557.
35. *Ibid.,* vol. LIII, no. 2, February 1859, p. 177.
36. *Ibid.,* vol. LI, December 1855, pp. 558–559.
37. *Ibid.,* vol. LVIII, no. 1, January 1859, p. 81.
38. *Ibid.,* vol. LV, no. 1, July 1857, p. 83.
39. *Ibid.,* vol. LIV, no. 5, May 1857, p. 468 and vol. LV, no. 2, August 1857, p. 179.
40. *Ibid.,* vol. LVIII, no. 1, January 1859, p. 81.
41. *Ibid.,* vol. LI, no. 5, November 1855, p. 468.
42. *Ibid.,* vol. L, no. 4, April 1855, p. 369.
43. *Ibid.,* vol. XLIX, no. 4, October 1854, p. 368 and vol. LII, no. 5, May 1856, p. 467.
44. *Ibid.,* vol. XLIX, no. 5, November 1854, p. 460.
45. *Ibid.,* vol. LXI, no. 4, October 1860, pp. 368–369.
46. *Ibid.,* vol. XLIX, no. 5, November 1854, p. 460.

his daughter at Paris, Kentucky,[47] and the Tennessee Female College at Franklin, Williamson County, Tennessee.[48] The Oread Institute of Worcester, Massachusetts, was considered a "Female Collegiate Seminary" with the "advantages of a collegiate course of study." [49]

The term was used to refer to a "business college" as Eastman's Mercantile College at Rochester,[50] the Pittsburgh Commercial College,[51] and Jonathan Jones' Commercial College of St. Louis, which provided a young man with "a footing as respectable as any in the University." [52] While business colleges were primarily for men, women seem to have been admitted.

In the "Editors' Table" for April 1855, Mrs. Hale stated that the *American Almanac of Useful Knowledge* for the year 1855 noted only one female college in the United States, the Wesleyan College of Macon, Georgia.[53] The American Women's Educational Association was formed in New York in 1852 under the leadership of Catharine Beecher "to secure a liberal education for their sex." It was instrumental in founding colleges for women in Milwaukee, Wisconsin and Dubuque, Iowa. These were endowed institutions which used the college plan of organization. Their aim and that of the American Women's Educational Association was to prepare girls for "the appropriate *profession* of woman, this profession being considered as embracing the training of the human mind, the care of the human body in infancy and sickness, and the conservation and domestic economy of the family state." [54] The Milwaukee Female College was chartered in 1851 and was known as a college in 1853 but did not

47. *Ibid.,* vol. XLVII, no. 1, July 1853, p. 85.
48. *Ibid.,* vol. LXI, no. 6, December 1860, p. 577.
49. *Gleason's Pictorial Drawing Room Companion,* vol. IV, no. 12, whole no. 90, March 19, 1853, p. 177.
50. *The Sibyl,* vol. III, no. XVI, February 15, 1859, p. 511.
51. *Pittsburgh Saturday Visiter,* vol. IV, no. XXXII, August 30, 1851, p. 127.
52. *The Western Journal of Agriculture, Manufacture, Mechanic Arts, Internal Improvement, Commerce and General Literature,* vol. II, no. VI, September 1849, pp. 439–440 (quotation p. 440); vol. VII, no. II, November 1851, fourth page of advertising section (not numbered).
53. *Godey's Lady's Book,* vol. L, no. 4, April 1855, p. 368.
54. *Ibid.,* vol. LI, no. 3, September 1855, pp. 276–277.

award the bachelor's degree until 1875.[55] When, in 1860, the Baltimore Female College honored Edward Everett for his work in behalf of the Mount Vernon Ladies' Association which purchased the home of Washington, Alexander H. Stephens "for his efforts in establishing a female college" in Georgia and "Mrs. Sarah Josepha Hale, the editress of *Godey's Lady's Book* for her distinguished service in the cause of female education," medals, not honorary degrees were given.[56] Many other female colleges were mentioned and described, as the Franklin Ladies' College of Holly Springs, Mississippi; [57] the Mississippi Ladies' College at Hernando, Mississippi, which was incorporated under the laws of the state of Mississippi; [58] the Wesleyan Female College of Cincinnati,[59] and the Ohio Female College at College Hill, Hamilton County, Ohio.[60]

But the first woman's college which the editors considered equal to those of men was Vassar.[61] They meant not the "fresh water" colleges, which themselves had a battle for recognition, but the long established colleges along the Atlantic seaboard. To the women of Philadelphia, Boston and New York, the admission of women to Antioch and Oberlin gave courage, hope and gratification; but with the opening of Vassar, during the Civil War, they felt they had arrived.[62] It was the first college for women not to be known as a

55. Woody, *op. cit.,* vol. I, p. 377.
56. *Godey's Lady's Book,* vol. LX, no. 6, June 1860, p. 557.
57. *Ibid.,* vol. LII, no. 6, December 1856, p. 559.
58. *Ibid.,* vol. LIV, no. 3, March 1857, p. 275.
59. *Ibid.,* vol. XLVII, no. 3, October 1853, p. 368.
60. *Ibid.,* vol. LIX, no. 1, July 1859, p. 83.
61. *Ibid.,* vol. LXI, no. 4, October 1860, pp. 368–369 and *Sibyl,* vol. IV, no. 18, March 15, 1860, p. 718; vol. IV, no. 21, May 1, 1860, p. 740.
62. According to Woody, *op. cit.,* vol. II, p. 184, "Mary Sharp (1851) was the earliest college for women only, in the United States, which required both Latin and Greek, though in meager amount, in a four year course, and gave an A.B. degree comparable both in form and significance, to those issued by men's colleges. . . . Elmira (1855) is the oldest existing women's college in the United States which succeeded in attaining standards in a fair degree comparable with men's colleges at the very beginning of her career. Vassar, ten years thereafter, likewise attained fairly comparable standards and was the first woman's college that was adequately endowed. Ten years later, Smith College formed the culmination of the effort to found 'a college like a man's . . . to teach them all that men are taught.' "

"female college." [63] Vassar was a victory in nomenclature and in academic standing.

These were two victories in which Mrs. Hale may have had a part, for she valiantly campaigned for college education for women and against the obnoxious use of the word, "female." [64] In fact, all the women editors, like the women educators, championed all kinds of education for women. Some men joined their crusade.

63. *Godey's Lady's Book,* vol. LXXIV, no. 4, April 1867, p. 374.
64. *Ibid.,* vol. IV, no. 2, August 1857, pp. 177–178.

CHAPTER SIX

Public Education

*I*N the crusades for free public education, editors of magazines for ladies and gentlemen were not content with description. Like the professional educational journals, they took definite leadership. This is not surprising, for the quarter of a century before the Civil War marked the rise of the common man. Legislation in the states had removed qualifications for suffrage, until in many Northern and Western states, all white, twenty-one-year-old males were eligible to vote. There were, of course, numerous exceptions. Pennsylvania was typical of the states, north and south, which required non-property owners to pay a poll tax. In Rhode Island the Freeman's Constitution of 1842 gave suffrage only to native-born American men. Despite such limitations, however, there was, in many states, by the middle of the nineteenth century, an approach to universal white, manhood suffrage. As the Constitution of the United States left to the states the determination of qualifications for suffrage, so by implication it left to the states and to the local governments control of education. In the early nineteenth century there was an even greater divergence among the states in the matter of free schools than in the qualifications for suffrage.

By 1800, New England, with the exception of Rhode Island, and New York provided for entire or for partial support of schools by taxation. The rate-bill system for paying for public education usually prevailed there. By this system, schools were established under public auspices, but the cost of instruction was seldom met entirely by the public treasury. The deficit thus incurred was divided among the pupils on a pro-rata basis and assumed by the parents. To the proud but poor citizen, inability to assume his children's share of the deficit was galling. Even more galling was the stigma of charity to the poor citizen of Pennsylvania or any of the other states which provided free education only for paupers. The rate-bill system and the pauper school were, however, important stepping stones on the path to free, public education.

The states carved from the Northwest Territory were able to omit such intermediate steps because they could utilize the educational provisions of the Ordinance of 1785 of the Congress under the Articles of Confederation and set aside definite sections of land for public schools. In contrast, Mississippi and Arkansas, which had a similar federal land grant system, had not, by the middle of the nineteenth century, availed themselves of this means of financing free schools. As suffrage was extended, public schools became free. In 1834, for example, a law providing for free public education was passed by the legislature of Pennsylvania, largely as a result of the extension of suffrage, the pressure of labor unions and the leadership of Thaddeus Stevens. Thus, movements for the establishment of free schools and the extension of suffrage dovetailed. As the non-propertied men gained the ballot, they increased free schools. Conversely, it was recognized that education was the chief means of securing an intelligent electorate.[1]

It is not surprising that the growth of free schools has been deemed the outstanding educational development of the period. Horace Mann and Henry Barnard were leaders in the movement. Numbers of educational journals were founded to support, improve, and bring information about the public schools.[2] The editors and publishers were frank in making their intentions known. The prospectus of *The Common School Assistant,* which catered to the state of New York, in 1831 announced:

The improvement of the Common Schools is the exclusive object of this paper. From statistical tables, it can be seen, that only one pupil in twenty goes higher than the common school. This paper, therefore, will endeavor to assist nineteen out of twenty, of the chil-

1. Eby and Arrowood, *op. cit.,* pp. 712–725; Knight, *op. cit.,* chs. VIII and IX; Noble, *op. cit.,* chs. IX and X; and Reisner, *op. cit.,* especially ch. XV.
2. *Common School Assistant* and *Common School Journal* were founded in 1836; *Connecticut Common School Journal,* in 1838; *The Common School Journal of the State of Pennsylvania,* in 1844.

dren of these United States, while they are acquiring the only education they are ever to receive.

The necessity of general knowledge and good morals, is admitted by every reflecting man; yet the great majority do not perceive, *that the Common Schools are the very sources of a nation's intelligence.* . . . They are at once *the sources and the guardians of freedom.* . . .[3]

Two years later, Henry Barnard informed "the Public" that the *Connecticut Common School Journal* would be "a periodical devoted to the great cause of popular education." [4] In 1846, the publisher of Horace Mann's *Common School Journal* noted in the first number of volume VIII that it was a source of comfort that the journal was "still alive," and the editor in thanking the subscribers stated:

. . . As we understand the subject of education better, we love and reverence it more. As we become more acquainted with its power and beneficence, we wish more earnestly that its kingdom may be extended, until it shall include all other kingdoms, and embrace the whole earth in its benign control. . . .[5]

It might seem as if the ladies' magazines and their literary contemporaries which deemed their circulation to be national would not discuss purely local questions. Such was not the case. While many editors failed to consider the political matter of suffrage, all united in their support of free schools. They used many of the same arguments as their professional contemporaries.

The basic argument for the public support of free schools was that free education was necessary, if the electorate were to be intelligent [6] and that democracy could function desirably only where the electorate was intelligent.[7] The direct connection between lack of education and undesirable voting was shown concretely in *Frank Leslie's Illustrated Newspaper.*

3. *Common School Assistant,* vol. I, no. 1, January 1836, pp. 1–4.
4. *Connecticut Common School Journal,* vol. I, no. 1, August 1838, p. 1.
5. *Common School Journal,* vol. VIII, no. 1, January 1, 1846, p. 2.
6. *National Magazine and Ladies' Emporium,* vol. I, no. 2, December 1830, pp. 137–138.
7. *Southern Literary Messenger,* vol. VII, no. 9, September 1841, pp. 631–637; *United States Magazine and Democratic Review,* vol. VIII, no. XXXIV, October 1840, pp. 360–366.

The Why and Wherefore—Indiana has gone stronger pro-slavery than any other Northern State. The white native citizens of Indiana, over twenty years of age, who could not read and write in 1850, numbered 69,445—greater than the same class numbered in any other State, north or south, except Virginia and North Carolina, and more than double the number New York contained, with three times the population. The vote in Indiana is thus accounted for. But the future promises well. The census from which we get the above facts shows that at the same time Indiana had 220,960 children attending school.[8]

The Southern Lady's Companion in January 1851, quoted at length a speech of Daniel Webster in which he showed the necessity of training for the wise exercise of the elective franchise.[9] A decade earlier a writer in the *Southern Literary Messenger* had made clear that the gradual extension of suffrage imposed "a solemn duty on all enlightened friends of liberty, to make corresponding efforts for extending the light of knowledge, and with it, that virtue which is its natural companion.[10] A member of the Keokuk, Iowa Bar, wrote at length for the *Western Journal* on "Government and Education" and pointed out that education was "peculiarly and emphatically the duty of the government." [11]

To many writers education for intelligent voting was not an end in itself but an aspect of preparation for intelligent citizenship. Through the opaque and verbose articles of M. Seneca in *The Lily* ran the theme that education "if diffused among the mass" would "do much to perpetuate liberty and equality." [12] As another writer put it, without education "man is not in any sense of the word a freeman." [13] Education was considered to be the chief means of im-

8. *Frank Leslie's Illustrated Newspaper*, vol. III, no. 53, December 13, 1856, p. 19.

9. *Southern Lady's Companion,* vol. 5, no. 10, January 1852, pp. 301–302.

10. *Southern Literary Messenger*, vol. VII, no. 9, September 1841, p. 631.

11. *The Western Journal of Agriculture, Manufacture, Mechanic Arts, Internal Improvement, Commerce and General Literature*, vol. VI, no. V, August 1851, pp. 309–319; no. VI, September 1851, pp. 356–357 (quotation from p. 314).

12. *The Lily*, vol. I, no. 11, November 1, 1849, p. 84.

13. *National Anti-Slavery Standard*, vol. 6, no. 27, December 1, 1845, p. 105.

proving society.[14] The relation between public schools and public good was clearly indicated in an editorial in *The Lily:*

. . . We regard them [public schools] as, under God, the affluent source of New England's enterprise and skill, her quiet and thrift, her safety at home and her honor abroad. They are the check and balance of power; the poor man's treasure, and the rich man's bond. —They are the eyes of liberty and the hands of law, as they are both the root and offspring of religion. . . .[15]

An English writer believed that the prosperity of America was due to the enlightenment of her people.[16]

Another aspect of the campaigns for free schools was to prove that they were worth the cost. Henry Barnard, Commissioner of Public Schools in Rhode Island, was quoted as having mentioned in the "Journal of Rhode Island Institute of Instruction" [17] that "the cost of the conflict [probably Dorr's Rebellion] taught the most parsimonious, that it was cheaper in a pecuniary respect to prevent than to defray the expenses incident to an uninstructed populace." [18] A writer, who pointed out the harm done in Virginia by confining state assistance to the education of paupers, showed clearly the responsibility of the state to provide free education for all.

. . . The diffusion of knowledge is clearly one of those great purposes for which all should be taxed for the common benefit of all. It is the right and duty of the government to take a portion of our property to secure the rest, as well as our lives and liberty, by military defense in war, and a wise and pure administration of justice in peace. Surely it cannot be denied that the State has an equal authority, and that it is equally politic to aid in the cultivation of those noble faculties which distinguish man from brutes, and which if properly improved, will create a security of property, and a national strength, which all the statute books, and all the fortification in existence,

14. *Southern Literary Messenger,* vol. VIII, no. 2, February 1842, pp. 114–121, and vol. XI, no. 10, October 1845, pp. 603–607.

15. *The Lily,* vol. 5, no. 23, December 1, 1853, p. 1.

16. Quoted from *Frazier's Magazine* in *Harper's New Monthly Magazine,* vol. I, no. II, July 1850, p. 209.

17. *North American Review,* vol. LXVII, no. CXL, July 1848, pp. 240–256.

18. *North American Review,* vol. LXVII, no. CXL, July 1848, p. 247.

cannot give. If it be, as it confessedly is, a public State interest, its benefits and burdens should be equally divided among all citizens. Not only those who have children to educate, but all classes and conditions should be made to sustain a system, which, if vigorously and judiciously supported, is worth a thousand militia systems for national defense; and is at least equal to the courts of justice for the preservation of life and property. When all have been thus made to bear a part of the burthen [sic], they of course will be admitted to an equal participation of the benefits, and the invidious distinction between pauper and non-pauper, be at once abolished. . . .[19]

In establishing a system of free education in a slave state, a writer in *DeBow's Review* felt that the state had no obligation to provide education for its "laboring class," but "that it *is* required to afford that degree of education to every one of its white citizens which will enable him intelligently and actively to control and direct the slave labor of the State." [20]

The value of publicly supported education was generally acknowledged by the editors. Mrs. Swisshelm believed that everybody knew the importance of free schools but that not one in a thousand felt it.[21] Mrs. Bloomer was one who felt it. In *The Lily* she described the Free School Convention, held at Syracuse July 10 and 11, 1850, noted that it was well attended and had been addressed by Horace Greeley and made this pertinent comment and clarion call:

The constitution of the new state of New Mexico just adopted, provides for the establishment of free schools in the embryo state. It would be a burning shame were the great state of New York, the oldest and most wealthy in the union to reject a principle which her youngest sister has so nobly proclaimed! Friends of free schools! do your whole duty and you will not fail to succeed. . . .[22]

19. *Southern Literary Messenger,* vol. VII, no. 9, September 1841, pp. 631–637.

20. *DeBow's Review and Industrial Resources, Statistics, etc.,* vol. XX, second series Vol. X, no. 2, February 1856, pp. 143–156; quotation p. 148.

21. *Pittsburgh Saturday Visiter,* vol. III, no. 11, March 30, 1850, p. 42.

22. *The Lily,* vol. 2, no. 8, August 1850, p. 61. (The nice distinction between a state and a territory was lost in enthusiasm for education.)

And do it they did. Mrs. Swisshelm with joy recorded, "There has been a signal triumph of free schools at the recent election in New York. The state canvass will show a majority *against* the repeal of free school laws of 50,000 to 100,000." [23] Later she gave the provisions of the New York School Bill.[24]

Despite their approval of free schools, there was divergence of opinion among the editors as to the kind of schools which should be publicly supported. Many believed that the state should provide only elementary education, just the key subjects, whereby the child might enter the portals of the temple of knowledge.[25] At the other extreme were the few who felt that education should be "treated as a whole," that the care of the state should be extended to every portion of it.[26] Editors campaigned for high schools for girls as well as boys,[27] for free colleges,[28] for publicly supported normal schools.[29] In fact there was no phase of education which at least one editor did not consider worthy of the support of the individual state or the whole nation. However, by and large, when non-professional writers of the mid-nineteenth century referred to "free schools" or "common schools" or "public schools," they meant elementary schools. Some professional educators held the same opinion.[30] So intrenched was this idea that it survives a century later in places along the Atlantic seaboard in the customary use of "public schools" to mean elementary schools.

Progress in the growth of these free schools was frequently noted. Statistics were cited to make this progress graphic. In June 1850, Mrs. Bloomer recorded that the "legislature of Mississippi had ap-

23. *Pittsburgh Saturday Visiter,* vol. III, no. 44, November 16, 1850, p. 174.
24. *Ibid.,* vol. IV, no. XV, May 5, 1851, p. 60.
25. *Southern Quarterly Review,* vol. XXV (new series vol. IX) no. XVIII, April 1854, pp. 475–476.
26. *Ibid.,* vol. XXX (new series vol. XI) no. 1, November 1856, p. 148.
27. *Godey's Lady's Book,* vol. XLVI, no. 2, February 1853, p. 176.
28. *Ibid.,* vol. XLVII, no. 2, August 1853, pp. 177–178.
29. *Ibid.,* vol. XLIV, no. 5, June 1852, pp. 511–515.
30. *Common School Assistant,* vol. I, no. 1, January 1836, pp. 1–4; *Common School Journal,* vol. I, no. 4, February 15, 1839, pp. 56–62; *Connecticut Common School Journal,* vol. I, no. 1, August 1838, p. 1.

propriated $200,000, for which the people were to be taxed, to be distributed among the several counties in proportion to the number of children, to establish a system of free schools." [31] Eight years later, Drs. Hasbrouck quoted from the *New York Daily Times* to show that more than three hundred public schools had opened in New York City and more than one hundred in Brooklyn.[32] "The prosperous and flourishing State of Ohio" boasted of "12,664 schools. Nearly $200,000 was paid by Ohio for common schools in the year 1851." [33] According to the "Editors' Table" of the *Lady's Book,* it was "stated on good authority that Rhode Island surpasses all other States in the Union for elegant and convenient school buildings. The improvements made in this department within a few years are gratifying evidence of the interest felt in the cause of universal education. This little State is thus gaining a wide and commanding influence in our Union, not only for furnishing the material helps of education, but also for the care the managers of the public schools exercise in providing excellent teachers. . . ." [34]

In the spring of 1859 the editor of the *Lady's Book* took occasion to review the "Progress of Popular Education in Pennsylvania" and gave her readers a clear picture of the growth and cost of the common school system.

When the Common School System was established in 1835 it numbered 762 schools, 808 teachers, and 32,000 scholars. The total expenses were about $305,775.

In 1858 we had 11,281 schools, 12,823 teachers; 569,880 scholars and the expenses were $2,138,038.

Though the expenditures of the system have been largely increased, tuition has in reality become much cheaper. In 1835, the average cost of teaching each scholar per month was $1.12½; in 1850, it had reached $1.44, since which year a gradual reduction took place, so that in 1858 it was no more than 53 cents. On the other hand has the average monthly salary for teachers, which was for male teachers only $18.34 and for female teachers $11.96 in 1836, been raised

31. *The Lily,* vol. II, no. 6, June 1850, p. 43.
32. *The Sibyl,* vol. III, no. 7, October 1, 1858, p. 435.
33. *Godey's Lady's Book,* vol. LII, no. 3, September 1852, p. 294.
34. *Ibid.,* vol. LIX, no. 5, November 1859, p. 467.

considerably, so that in 1858 it amounted to $24.25 for the former and $17.22 for the latter. In 1835, the schools were open only three months and twelve days. The time has been prolonged gradually, so that in 1858 they were kept open five months and twenty-five days. These are certainly most satisfactory results, showing a growing appreciation, on the part of the public, of the educational system, as well as the capacities of the latter for good.[35]

Statistics for school attendance in Pennsylvania, exclusive of Philadelphia, were given in the *Pittsburgh Saturday Visiter*.[36] It was noted in the *Ladies' Repository* that, in 1852, 832,481 children had attended public schools in New York state; 480,798 in Pennsylvania.[37] In "Education in the United States," the editor of *Gleason's Pictorial* noted that there were about 60,000 supported by an annual expense of about six millions of dollars, a condition which he considered would give "little cause for boasting, though much for hope."[38]

Reports of Boards of Education were reprinted with comment. *The Southern Quarterly Review* in Charleston, South Carolina, printed the "Thirty-Second Annual Report of the Controllers of the Public Schools of the City and County of Philadelphia for Year Ending June 30, 1850"[39] and Horace Mann's report on the schools of Massachusetts.[40] Horace Mann's reports were frequently quoted.[41] The Report of the Commissioners of the Common Schools in Connecticut[42] and that of the Superintendent of the Common Schools of Pennsylvania[43] also appeared. Descriptions of schools were given,

35. *Ibid.*, vol. LVIII, no. 4, April 1859, p. 370.
36. *Pittsburgh Saturday Visiter*, vol. III, no. 3, February 2, 1850, p. 10.
37. *Ladies' Repository*, vol. XIII, no. 3, March 1853, p. 139.
38. *Gleason's Pictorial Drawing-Room Companion*, vol. VII, no. 16, whole no. 172, October 21, 1854, p. 253.
39. *Southern Quarterly Review*, vol. XX, whole no. 40, new series vol. IV, no. 8, October 1851, pp. 480–490.
40. *Ibid.*, vol. VI, no. XII, October 1844, pp. 453–482; vol. VII, no. 13, January 1845, pp. 1–74.
41. *North American Review*, vol. LIX, no. CXXV, October 1844, pp. 329–352; *Home Journal*, series for 1847, no. 7, whole no. 53, February 13, 1847, p. 2 (not numbered).
42. *North American Review*, vol. LIV, no. CXV, April 1842, pp. 458–476.
43. *Pittsburgh Saturday Visiter*, vol. III, no. 3, February 2, 1850, p. 10.

as that of the fifteenth ward School for Girls which could accommodate 1600 but in 1856 had only 785 pupils and cost $67,500 (lot $22,500 and building $45,000).[44]

The work of the public schools was both criticized and appreciated. The "Editor's Table" of *Harper's* for March 1860 had an interesting, illuminating, and sympathetic discussion on "Our Schools."

The part of a machine that attracts most attention is usually that which is most out of order. . . . These schools themselves, indeed sometimes become matters of popular agitation, and our politicians find in them new charms or fears the moment that some partisan or sectional question disturbs their administration, and some feud as to a book, a teacher, or a committee sets the town agog, and is made to furnish capital for the next election. But what is best in our school system, its quiet, comprehensive, effective working, is but little known and appreciated, and although perhaps boasted of sufficiently in speeches of the spread-eagle order and in Fourth of July orations, its worth is very little realized. The statistics of our American popular education are marvelous, and their plain figures numerical make ambitious figures of speech needless. What can be more eloquent than the fact that little Massachusetts has over two hundred thousand children in her common schools, and spends yearly a million and a half dollars upon their education; and that great New York has more than eight hundred thousand scholars, and spends upon them over three million a year; while youthful Ohio gathers into her schools over six hundred thousand children, at a cost of over two million. These figures rise in importance when it is remembered that they imply not so much the votes of great public assemblies or centralized authority, as the action of the people themselves in towns and districts, and that our system generally carries our method of local responsibility and popular liberty to its extreme limit. Each township, and often each school district, appoints its own teachers and raises its own funds; while each State now tends to have some central supervision over the schools, and the best policy favors a central Board of Education with an effective secretary, yet the democratic feeling invariably sets some limit to the supervision, and

44. *Frank Leslie's Illustrated Newspaper*, vol. II, no. 27, June 14, 1856, p. 13.

reserves wholesome rights to the townships and districts. This system is, on the whole, the most consistent and remarkable fruit of our American liberty, because it combines so much freedom and so much order, showing us millions of children gathered together generally under a very strict discipline, yet with popular approbation and support. So far as order is concerned, the free schools are more exemplary than the private schools, and the many who send their children to the master of the district are found to be less fault-finding and capricious than the few who seek for their more exacting children more select schools. Sometimes, indeed, refractory parents disturb teachers in their just discipline, but generally the citizens at large take the conservative side, and a firm and judicious method is quite sure of having the support of the people. Certainly the acquiescence of our young republic in this vast system of school government is more memorable and cheering, and we are willing to compare the annals of the last thirty years of our popular education with any intellectual movement within the history of civilization. . . .[45]

On the whole, editors viewed with pride the growth of free schools. Many felt that since elementary schools had proved their worth, free high schools, colleges, normal schools and evening schools for workers would likewise be worth while. The advantages of the public high school were stated in the *Journal of Rhode Island Institute of Instruction*. The work would be better done than in the district schools. It made suitable provision for advanced pupils of both sexes. It equalized the opportunities of a good education and brought the provisions of a good school within the reach of all classes of the community. The annual or semi-annual examination for entrance to high school would stimulate the teachers and pupils in the lower schools. The aggregate expense for education, including private and public schools would be decreased, although the expense to the taxpayer might be increased. The public high school would help create a better sentiment in favor of public schools. The article concluded with a series of testimonials from the principals of the high schools in Boston, Worcester, Brattleboro, and the High School for Girls at

45. *Harper's New Monthly Magazine,* vol. XX, no. CXVIII, March 1860, pp. 550–555.

Newburyport. Such testimonials the writer felt could be obtained from Philadelphia and Lowell.[46]

The Central High School of Philadelphia was described in the *American Journal of Education* [47] and *Sartain's Union Magazine*.[48] High school education for boys was considered desirable.

The higher education for girls was a very different matter. In an editorial in the first number of her *Ladies' Magazine,* Mrs. Hale expressed regret at "the recent suspension of the public High School for Girls in Boston" and hoped "that it will still be found practicable to remove all obstacles to its reestablishment upon an enlarged and permanent foundation. Let our cities and populous towns," she continued, "establish seminaries of this description within their own limits, and our legislators will soon be induced to establish them throughout the country." [49] Later, Miss Anthony regretted the exclusion of girls from "higher educational institutions, supported by the State." [50]

In 1853 Mrs. Hale began her campaign for a high school for girls in Philadelphia.

High School for Girls— In many of our cities, "High Schools for Boys" are established and sustained in the most liberal manner; but in all the land, there is but one institution of the kind for girls which is at Providence, Rhode Island. Honor be to the State of Roger Williams, where liberty of conscience was first established! It now leads the way to enlightening the world, for never can men be wise till women are well instructed.

Philadelphia has one of the most flourishing High Schools for Boys in the United States. It is deservedly the pride and the boast of the city. Five hundred boys are now in their course of training in this High School. Where is its twin seminary for the daughters of the people? Are these, the jewels of the State, the grace and glory

46. *Journal of Rhode Island Institute of Instruction,* vol. III, no. 1, January 1848, pp. 253–259.

47. *American Journal of Education,* vol. I, no. 1, August 1855, pp. 93–102.

48. *Sartain's Union Magazine of Literature and Art,* vol. VIII, no. 4, April 1851, pp. 286–287.

49. *The Ladies' Magazine,* vol. I, no. 1, January 1828, p. 23.

50. *The Sibyl,* vol. IV, no. IV, August 15, 1859, p. 607.

of their homes, to be forgotten, and left in comparative ignorance, when the character and destiny of the coming generation are to be in their keeping?

We do not believe this important subject will be much longer overlooked, and we will venture to commend it to the earnest attention of the good people of Philadelphia, women as well as men. Surely mothers should have a deep interest in the education of their daughters. If the women of this city would address a memorial to the Legislature now in session, asking for a "High School for Girls" similar in its advantages to that for "Boys," should be established here, would there be any serious opposition to the measure? We trust not. The experiment is at least worth trying.[51]

The editor of the *Lady's Book* was not content with one attack. Five months later as part of an article on the enlargement of woman's sphere by the use of the needle, she wrote, . . . "Would not a Female High School do this? Yes, the High School for Girls! that is what Philadelphia lacks and must have before the city attains her highest eminence. Educate the girls properly and the world will see a better and nobler race of men." [52] Not quite a year later she renewed her plea.[53] In August, 1854, in her "Editors' Table," she wrote, "Make way for Boston. The City Councils of Boston have proposed that four High Schools for Girls shall be established in that city, having at the head of such a lady of the highest accomplishments. Should this liberal provision for female education be made, the old Puritan City will shine forth with a new lustre in the 'good time coming.' " [54] The following May she continued her effort in behalf of a high school for girls. "Free Academy for Girls— The liberal men of New York are about establishing another institution similar to the 'Free Academy for Boys' for the benefit of the daughters of their city. When is the 'High School for Girls' to be established in Philadelphia?" [55] Ten years later the editor of the *Lady's Book* could point with pride.

51. *Godey's Lady's Book,* vol. XLVI, no. 2, February 1853, p. 170.
52. *Ibid.,* vol. XLVII, no. 1, July 1853, p. 84.
53. *Ibid.,* vol. XLVIII, no. 5, May 1854, p. 464.
54. *Ibid.,* vol. LXIX, no. 2, August 1854, p. 176.
55. *Ibid.,* vol. L, no. 5, May 1855, p. 468.

THE GIRLS' HIGH SCHOOL AND THE YOUNG LADIES' NORMAL SCHOOL
are two institutions of which Philadelphia may well be proud. The
schools are liberally supported, and have a first rate corps of teachers; both men and women have places as instructors. At the last Commencement, which was in June, forty young ladies graduated from
these two schools. The courses of study are thorough, all the branches
of an English education required for young men in their profession
are learned—we were about to say *mastered*—by these young ladies,
who are trained to teach in the common schools where boys will be
under their instruction.[56]

Mrs. Hale was the most persistent of the women editors in champion-
ing the cause of the public high school for girls. She also advocated
the publicly financed normal school. In this effort, she was joined by
Mrs. Davis and Mrs. Swisshelm. Mrs. Swisshelm advocated state support for normal schools; [57] Mrs. Hale, federal.[58]

The campaigns for free education on the college level and for the
use of public funds for the support of colleges admitting women
were far less successful than that for either high schools for girls
or normal schools. Mrs. Davis considered it selfish savageism that
among "two hundred fifty institutions of learning in its higher grades,
supported both by private munificence and state governments, not
above half a dozen" admitted women.[59] W. B. S., writing six years
earlier on "The Claims of Woman" in *The Southern Lady's Companion,* suggested that half the public funds for education be ap-
propriated for female improvement and progress and that each
state "erect a college for its daughters, as well as for its sons." [60]

In 1853, Mrs. Hale jubilantly burst forth:

56. *Ibid.,* vol. LXXI, no. 3, September 1865, p. 266. The Normal School
for Girls was opened officially on January 13, 1848 and was reorganized as
a Girls' High School June 9, 1859. In February 1860 diplomas were granted
to thirty graduates of the Girls' High School. These facts may be found
on page 36 of Robert Wayne Clark's *The Genesis of the Philadelphia High
School for Girls,* a thesis for the degree of D.Ed. at Temple University,
published in Philadelphia in 1938.
57. *Pittsburgh Saturday Visiter,* vol. III, no. 48, December 14, 1850, p. 190.
58. See chapter VII.
59. *The Una,* vol. III, no. 8, August 1855, p. 121.
60. *Southern Lady's Companion,* vol. III, no. 8, Nov. 1849, pp. 169–173.

Pennsylvania for Woman— This noble old State is now taking the lead in the movement so important to the real progress of humanity. Here the right of married women to hold property is liberally secured; here the first Female Medical College has been chartered with powers and rights as ample as those given to male institutions and now *a real bona fide college for women is chartered;* and thus wisely the Editor (foot-note: Professor Charles E. Blumenthal) of "The Temple," a Masonic periodical, discourses concerning the matter:— ". . . Such an institution has long been a desideratum. The present state of society requires that the daughters who are destined to become the wives of the young men educated under the existing advanced state of education, should themselves have a share of that education. Those who are desirous of preparing themselves to become teachers, or to take some other active share in the busy scenes of life, have now an institution opened to them, where a thorough course can be pursued to whatever branch of academic education, they wish to perfect themselves." . . .

Mrs. Hale noted the value of the central location at Harrisburg; quoted the bill; and cited the sponsors who included Luther Reily, Superintendent of the Common Schools of Pennsylvania.[61]

A year later she, again, gave her "warm approval" to "the establishment of *Pennsylvania Female College at Harrisburg."* Since she realized that "every one of the 300,000 persons who will read this number must be gratified to know the friends of women in the Keystone State," she listed the names of those interested; and quoted extensively from the Commencement Address of T. R. Tyson, which had been published by the trustees.[62]

About the same time, Mrs. Bloomer in *The Lily* championed the

61. *Godey's Lady's Book,* vol. XLVII, no. 2, August 1853, pp. 177–178.
62. *Ibid.,* vol. XLIX, no. 5, November 1854, pp. 458–459. The Pennsylvania Female College at Harrisburg was begun as a private school for girls by Mrs. Anna LeConte in 1849; it attained a high rank. In 1853 it was chartered by the state as a college. It was not a "public" institution; but since one of the sponsors was the Superintendent of Public Instruction and since Mrs. Hale considered it the creation of the state, it illustrates her belief that college education for girls should be provided by the state. The college closed about 1867. A brief account may be found in James Pyle Wickersham's *A History of Education in Pennsylvania,* Inquirer Publishing Company, Lancaster, Pa., 1886, p. 463.

cause of the People's College in the state of New York. In October,
1852 she commented upon it in a two-column editorial; noted that it
was "proposed to devise a new system whereby the laborer may be
educated with the means he has in his possession—a system that will
reach in its beneficent effects even the humblest citizen . . ." and
that it was supported by such people as Governor Hunt, Horace
Greeley and T. C. Peters, Esq., editor of the *Wool Grower*.[63] In
November, she gave a full page account, quoted largely from the
New York Tribune, of the People's College Meeting, where the
resolution was passed, "That the first and paramount object of a
College System should be, not only to give the student a full, clear
and accurate knowledge of the physical laws by which the universe
is governed, but also to teach the best practical application of those
laws to the work of the artisan and agriculturalist." In October,
1853, she called attention to the "proposed Educational Institution
in this State, known as the 'People's College' " and "strongly recommended it to public favor." She noted that the charter had been
obtained at the last session of the legislature and that it would
combine "Study with Labor, . . . Science with Industry." [64]

That a state college would stimulate the growth of common schools,
was a point made by F. A. P. Barnard in "Improvements Practicable
in American Colleges; a paper read before the American Association
for the Advancement of Education at its Fifth Annual Session"
which was reviewed and discussed in the *Southern Quarterly Review*. A state college was shown to be of benefit to the state in that
it provided enlightened men who would not be satisfied until a great
system of common schools was put into operation.[65]

The Home Journal commented favorably upon the opening of

63. *The Lily,* vol. 4, no. 10, October 1852, p. 87.
64. *Ibid.,* vol. 5, no. 19, October 1, 1853, p. 2. An account of the People's
College is given in Sidney Sherwood's *The University of the State of New
York,* United States Bureau of Education, 1900, vol. 3, Washington, Government Printing Office, 1900, pp. 320–323. The People's College was the
outcome of a movement begun as early as 1850. In 1851 an association was
formed to further the enterprise. It got land grant scrip, which, after a
lapse of two or three years it lost, because of failure to meet requirements.
65. *Southern Quarterly Review,* vol. 29 (new series, vol. 1) no. 1, April
1856, pp. 168–188.

public evening schools in New York.[66] In fact, only one proposal,
that of public support of a sectarian institution, did not meet with
editorial approval. Mrs. Swisshelm cited the demand of the *Pittsburgh Catholic* for the use of public funds for Catholic schools and
commented:

For one we should heartily oppose such division of the school fund.
We have quite enough caste and class—bitter sectarian prejudices
and religious hates now, without establishing public schools to foster
these particular branches of education. . . . Every attempt to
separate public schools according to sects, castes and classes should
be crushed in the bud.[67]

Editors of German magazines wished public support of German
speaking schools, including German high schools.[68] There was, however, no reflection of this desire in general magazines. With these two
exceptions, popular periodicals like professional journals advocated
public support of all kinds of education, college, normal school, high
school and evening school as well as elementary. While many of the
writers were not so blandiloquent as Charles D. Drake in his address,
entitled "The Grand Army of the American Public Schools," at the
dedication of the St. Louis High School, they none the less saw the
saga which he thus depicted:

. . . a vast host of four millions of boys and girls, buoyant with
youthful spirits, rosy with the bloom of health, radiant with happiness, bright with intelligence; walking, running, leaping, dancing,
jumping, playing, singing, shouting, as issuing from their millions
of homes, they march away with dashing steps, upon the beaten
street, along the winding road, by meadow-skirted paths, through the
silky corn, among the flowery cotton fields, beneath the orange groves,
by the rows of sugar cane, through the pebbly streams, out of the unhewn forest, over the prairies; by ocean, lake and river; from the
cabin, from the farm-house, from the laborer's plain abode, from the

66. *Home Journal,* whole no. 561, series for 1856, no. 45, November 8, 1856,
p. 3.
67. *Pittsburgh Saturday Visiter,* vol. III, no. 36, September 21, 1850,
p. 142.
68. *Atlantis,* neue Folge, Band 3, Heft 4, Oktober 1855, pp. 279–284.

splendid mansion; poor and rich, native and foreign-born, the humble
and the aspiring, all free and equal; meeting, greeting, kindly mingling, and gathering numbers as they go; big with purposes, flush
with joy, ever hopeful, breathing quick with life's young vigor, lithe
and hardy, gay and beautiful; on they go, the youthful army! East-
ward, Westward, Northward, Southward, in all the land their voice
is heard, their tread is felt, and their goings are watched by loving
eyes, and followed by yearning hearts, as they forward move, more
powerful for good than ever was marshalled columns for ill; . . .
the hope of our country is in motion; the youth of the nation is on its
way to be taught how to govern itself hereafter. . . . These are our
conscripts—the willing conscripts of education; this is the grand
army of the American Public Schools.[69]

"The Grand Army of the American Public Schools" was in a very
real sense the creation of the period, 1830–1860. In the 1830's, Mann
and Barnard gave impetus and direction to the crusade for public
schools. All the editors supported unstintingly the call to the crusade. While a vaster host than that seen by Drake in 1856 was yet to
form "the willing conscripts of education," public education, "the
hope of our country" was surely "set in motion" by 1860.

69. *Moore's Western Lady's Magazine,* vol. XIV, October 1856, pp. 113–
114.

CHAPTER SEVEN

Normal Schools and the Training of Teachers

*T*HE universal acceptance of the principle that elementary education should be public and free forced upon educators and laymen alike an appreciation of the need for good teaching. To educators, a good teacher was trained. In 1823, Samuel R. Hall opened probably the first normal school in the United States and urged that men be "educated for the business of teaching." [1] In 1831, T. H. Gallaudet in his "Remarks on Seminaries for Teachers" [2] made the same point. Horace Mann [3] and Henry Barnard [4] were leaders in the movement for teacher training. Educational journals participated in the campaign. [5] Men, interested in the profession of education, universally accepted the desirability and necessity of training for that profession. They appealed for the professional training of teachers at the same time they were campaigning for the common school.

They did not need to go far afield to secure evidence of poor teaching. Until 1830 it was the custom to hire as teachers men, who had been unsuccessful in other fields of endeavor, or recent gradu-

1. Quoted in Knight, *op. cit.,* p. 309.
2. *American Annals of Education and Instruction and Journal of Literary Institutions, being a continuation of the American Journal of Education,* vol. I, third series, no. 1, January 1831, pp. 24–30.
3. *Common School Journal,* vol. I, no. 6, March 15, 1839, p. 83; vol. V, no. 3, February 1843, p. 39, vol. VI, no. 17, September 2, 1844, pp. 265–268.
4. Henry Barnard, *Normal Schools and Other Institutions, Agencies, and Means, Designed for the Education of Teachers* (Hartford, 1851, 435 pp.); *Connecticut Common School Journal,* vol. III, no. 17, February 1, 1841, pp. 90–91; vol. XI (n.s. vol. III), no. 6, February 1856, pp. 38–40.
5. See 2, 3, and 4, and *American Journal of Education,* vol. III, no. IX, June 1857, pp. 416–427; *Common School Assistant,* vol. I, no. 11, November 1836, pp. 86–87; *The Pennsylvania School Journal,* vol. V, no. 11, May 1857, pp. 361–363.

ates or students of the academies or colleges, who tarried a year or two in the class-room before entering upon more lucrative work. Of course this mode of securing teachers did not cease in 1830. Even before 1830 there were trained teachers,—teachers trained in the model schools of the followers of Joseph Lancaster.[6] These men and women knew how to drill their little charges in the minimum essentials of knowledge.

Normal Schools probably arose as the result of the felt need for trained teachers. In the development of these schools, leaders of education and controllers of schools used the means at hand. Hall called his normal school a "seminary." Later he added teacher training to the Phillips Academy at Andover.[7] Normal schools in this country were rooted in the academy [8] and in the academy's free equivalent, the public high school. But there were other roots. Accounts of the Prussian Normal Schools by such men as Calvin E. Stowe and Henry Barnard influenced their development.[9] Again, as in the Philadelphia Normal School, there were roots in the humble Lancastrian model school as well as in the high school.[10]

Until 1830 almost all teachers were men. With the increase in common schools in succeeding decades, educators and laity alike realized that if there was to be universal, free, elementary education, paid for from the public treasury, there must be more teachers but the wages that the individual teacher received must be lower. At a time when a farm awaited almost any man and growing industry afforded countless opportunities, such a supply of teachers could be recruited only among girls and women. Some educators as Mann and Barnard considered women better teachers of little children than men.[11] Consequently the question of Normal Schools and teacher training was intimately bound up with the need of "female" education. The three great educational reforms,—common schools,

6. *The Southern Review,* vol. 1, no. 2, May 1828, pp. 478–502, article entitled "On the Monitorial System of Instruction" and Clark, *op. cit.,* p. 13.
7. Willard S. Elsbree, *The American Teacher* (New York, American Book Company, 1939, ix, 566 pp.) p. 145.
8. *Common School Journal,* vol. I, no. 6, March 15, 1839, p. 83, ". . . Normal Schools in New York engrafted on the academy . . ."
9. Knight, *op. cit.,* p. 315.   10. Clark, *op. cit.,* p. 13.
11. Elsbree, *op. cit.,* pp. 199 ff.

normal schools and education of women are so intertwined that it is difficult for the modern reader to unravel them. Contemporary editors of educational journals and popular periodicals made no such effort.

There was no agreement on the financing of normal schools. To those who saw them as an outgrowth of the academy or as an opportunity for girls to receive higher education, they should be financed at least in part by private means. To those, like Horace Mann, who saw them as a means to prepare teachers for the common schools, they should be publicly financed. Mann was instrumental in the opening of the first state normal school at Lexington, Massachusetts, on July 3, 1839.[12] In 1848, Philadelphia opened a city supported normal school.[13] City normal schools were opened in St. Louis (1857) and New Orleans (1858). By 1860 there were state normal schools in Massachusetts, Connecticut, New York, Pennsylvania, Illinois and Michigan. There were in 1860, thirteen publicly supported normal schools in the United States.[14]

Another aspect of the education of teachers was the training of teachers in service, through books and magazines for teachers and through Teachers' Institutes and Conventions. These phases of professional education were presented in the magazines for ladies and the literary periodicals.

The value of preparation for teaching had long been appreciated. As early as 1829, Mrs. Hale wrote on her "favorite project," the desirability of young ladies preparing themselves to be teachers.[15] *The Southern Rose* in 1835 noted that normal schools had originated in Prussia during the reign of Frederick the Great and that there were fifty-eight normal schools in that country.[16] In 1853, "A Lady" in "Thoughts on Normal Schools" [17] suggested that "benevolent

12. *Ibid.*, p. 146.   13. Clark, *op. cit.*, p. 36.
14. This information was obtained from "Table VII Statistics of Normal Schools in the United States, compiled from the Most Recent Reports sent to the United States Bureau of Education" in *Report of the Commissioner of Education*, Washington, Government Printing Office, 1870, pp. 526–527.
15. *The Ladies' Magazine*, vol. II, no. II, February 1829, pp. 91–92.
16. *Southern Rose*, vol. 3, no. 20, July 25, 1835, p. 190.
17. *Godey's Lady's Book*, vol. XLVI, no. 4, April 1853, pp. 302–303.

ladies of cultivated minds, and possessing means, who desire to do good beyond the immediate circle of the fireside, yet shrink from publicity, might endow such a school." [18]

Yet it was recognized that a teacher's worth depended "upon native aptitude as well as especial training." He needed "peculiar gifts" which "kind providence" supplied "in due proportion to the demand." [19] The teacher was "one of God's agents for the performance of a great and noble work"; [20] the preacher and the teacher were "God's chief agents in the intellectual, moral, and social advancement of the world." [21] Teaching was, in fact, "second only to the office of the sacred ministry." The faithful teacher should be "punctual, true and conscientious in the discharge of his duty," he should believe that he had a mission to fulfill and teach his pupils "by precept and example." [22]

In a less lofty but thoroughly practical way, the editors of the ladies' magazines promoted teaching as a desirable employment for a young lady. Mrs. Hale insisted that women made the best teachers and in 1830 in the *Ladies' Magazine* and in 1848 in *Godey's Lady's Book* printed her article, "Woman the Teacher." [23] The editors presented stories in which the heroine was a teacher. In 1844, *Godey's Lady's Book* offered the story of a teacher who had been deserted by her lover but who, through patience and self-sacrifice, triumphed over the "fractious humours of her pupils." [24] Mrs. S. C. Hall in "The Teacher" in *Miss Leslie's Magazine* made the teacher an even more acceptable Victorian heroine. She befriended a little Indian girl who had been left by her father in a fashionable school. From Ada "he learned how deep his debt of gratitude was to 'the teacher,' nor was he forgetful. The nabob is a widower, and there

18. *Ibid.*, p. 303.

19. *Harper's New Monthly Magazine,* vol. XX, no. CXCIII, March 1860, p. 552.

20. *Ibid.*, vol. XVIII, no. CIV, January 1859, pp. 261–266 (quotation p. 262).

21. *Ibid.*, p. 266.

22. *Ladies' Repository,* vol. XIII, no. 4, April 1853, p. 166.

23. *Godey's Lady's Book,* vol. XXXVII, no. 3, September 1848, pp. 143–144.

24. *Ibid.*, vol. XXIX, no. 5, November 1844, p. 194.

have been rumors abroad during the past month that Miss Graham is not to be established in a school but as mistress of his house. . . ." [25] Ten years later, Esther M. Sidney in "The Young Teacher" made her heroine, an orphan, achieve similar success.[26] The report that Mrs. Okill of New York City had made a quarter of a million dollars from her school may have enticed a few of the more mercenary; but Mrs. Hale, after mentioning the fact, set her readers straight as to the proper attitude. "We congratulate Mrs. Okill," she wrote, "not that she is rich, but that her services in the cause of education have been appreciated and rewarded." [27]

The women editors were not content with simply making teaching an attractive occupation for young ladies. Descriptions and reports of the National Popular Education Association, an association "formed for the purpose of sending female teachers from the Eastern States, where education of young ladies is best provided for, to the West and Southwestern portion of our land, where such instructors are wanted," were given. Under the auspices of the association, 248 teachers, chiefly from New England and New York had gone forth "as follows: 69 to Indiana; 69 to Illinois; 24 to Wisconsin; 18 to Michigan; 13 to Ohio; 12 to Iowa; 10 to Missouri; 8 to Tennessee; 5 to Pennsylvania; 3 to Minnesota; 3 to Kentucky; 3 to North Carolina; 3 to Alabama; 2 to Texas; 5 to Oregon; and one to the Shawnee Mission, destined to New Mexico." [28]

While the training of teachers under private auspices was deemed desirable, the editors believed that teachers for the public schools should be trained at public expense. In 1837 a review of *Thoughts on Popular and Liberal Education* by Dr. Charles Caldwell pointed out the nobility of the cause of education, the deplorable condition of education and the need for the education of teachers by the state.

. . . But Popular Education in the United States, on which the moral, intellectual and political soundness of the country so essen-

25. *Miss Leslie's Magazine,* vol. I, no. 1, January 1843, pp. 35–37.
26. *Peterson's Ladies' National Magazine,* vol. XXVI, no. 5, December 1854, pp. 376–381.
27. *Godey's Lady's Book,* vol. LI, no. 1, July 1855, p. 83.
28. *Ibid.,* vol. XLIV, no. 5, June 1852, pp. 511–515.

tially depends, is in a deplorable condition. Three or four states perhaps excepted, this is true of the Union. And even of the excepted states, it is true to an extent sufficiently ominous. The reason is plain. Except in the cities, and a few of the larger towns of the Union, the teachers of *primary schools* are as unfit for their vocation as imagination can conceive. This want of knowledge and letters, manners, dignity and character can hardly be surpassed. They are therefore disqualified alike to instruct and govern, set example and command respect. In truth they are disqualified for everything connected with education; because they are wholly uneducated themselves. Too indolent to labor with their hands, and too ignorant or feeble-minded to be concerned in business where intellect and knowledge are requisite, they become "school-masters," and teach their scholars bad English, bad habits, bad manners and too often bad morals. . . .[29]

Mrs. Swisshelm, in an editorial in 1850, was equally crystal clear, if not scathing, on this point.

Normal Schools . . . If the legislature does not take some steps to supply the Common Schools with teachers, it had better abolish the system entirely; or pass an act to unite the school and poor taxes, let them be distributed among the "deserving poor," and the guardians appoint the more able bodied paupers to take charge of the schools.

It is notorious that it is common practice in this State for men who can or will do nothing else—because they are poor—to induce some friend to recommend them to a board of directors, and these directors after having no choice, or only a choice of evils give heed to those recommendations, and in consequence our school funds are about as often given in charity, as for "reward of merit." . . . The art of teaching should be learned as well as any other art. Our school system now is a mockery, and it will never be much better until we have Normal Schools.[30]

Mrs. Hale waged an almost solitary and an unsuccessful campaign for the federal support of free normal schools for the training

29. *The Western Monthly Magazine and Literary Journal,* new series, vol. I, no. 3, April 1837, pp. 197–207 (quotation pp. 201–202).

30. *Pittsburgh Saturday Visiter,* vol. III, no. 48, December 14, 1850, p. 190.

of women teachers. She opened her campaign in June of 1852 with a
five page article in the *Lady's Book*. First, she established the point
that women were better teachers of little children than men, by
showing that "the Creator specially confided the care of the young
to woman," by indicating "that female influence should be paramount, from infancy to youth over sons as well as daughters."
Moreover, men were "not fitted by nature to be teachers of the
young" and every good man "bore testimony to the worth of female
influence and teaching in forming his character." Because so little
had been done for female education, "the Educator" was "left uneducated." Mrs. Hale naturally questioned the wisdom of such a condition. Next she cited statistics to show that female teachers far
outnumbered male teachers, eight to one in Philadelphia, for example, and that women teachers from New England and New York
were doing a splendid work in the West and Southwest. The crux
of the argument for free normal schools centered about the need of
universal education which no "reflecting mind" would doubt. About
5,000,000 of the population of 1852 were between the ages of five
and twenty and it was this group, Mrs. Hale believed, which would
determine the future of our country. In view of these facts, Mrs. Hale
suggested a new plan:

. . . On behalf of the patrons of the "Lady's Book," who represent the true cause of woman in our republic, we present the following *Petition to the Honorable Senate and House of Representatives
in Congress Assembled:*— That from the foregoing facts and statements, showing the importance of woman's agency in the instruction
of the young, and the pressing need of Female Teachers in the
Common Schools throughout the land, we venture to request that
your honorable body would make some provision for the suitable
education of these young ladies who are willing to become teachers,
if the way is open to them.

We respectfully ask the attention of Congress to the subject. While
the public domain is parceled out and granted for internal improvements and plans of national aggrandizement, we would humbly suggest that a small portion be set apart and allotted for the benefit
of the Daughters of the Republic. Three or four millions of acres

of land would be sufficient to found and endow one Free Normal
School for the education of Female Teachers in every State of the
Union.

These institutions could be modeled and managed in each state to
suit the wishes of its inhabitants, and young ladies of every section
would be trained as instructors for children in their own vicinity.
This would be found of immense advantage to the States where
schools have hitherto been neglected. In short, the value of all the
physical improvements in our country will be immeasurably enhanced
by the provision for Female Education; because in the influence of
intelligent and pure-minded women lies the moral power which alone
can give safety and permanence to our institutions, prosperity and
glory to our nation.[31]

In August 1852, Mrs. Hale enlarged on the project of federally subsidized but state controlled normal schools for girls, cited the petition to Congress, was "happy to record" that it had "met with kind
approbation" and in her own inimitable way marshalled the arguments in support of the petition.

1st Now two million, at least, of children and youth in the United
States are nearly destitute of school instruction, requiring at the
moment 20,000 additional teachers, if we give to each instructor the
care of one hundred pupils, quite too many for any common school
with only one teacher.

2d That to find 20,000 young men, who would enter the office
of pedagogue, would be utterly impossible, while the Great West, the
mines of California, and the open ocean laving China and the East,
are inviting them to adventure and activity.

3d That, therefore, young women must become teachers of the
common schools, or these must be given up. . . .

4th That young women make the best teachers has been proved
(see Reports of the Board of Popular Education and Reports of
Common Schools in Mass.)

5th Female teachers are now largely employed, on an average
of six of these to one male teacher, in New England, New York,
Pennsylvania, Ohio, and wherever the common school system is
in a prospering condition; and everywhere these teachers are found
faithful and useful.

31. *Godey's Lady's Book,* vol. XLIV, no. 5, June 1852, pp. 511–515.

6th That, to make education *universal,* it must be *moderate in expense,* and women can afford to teach for one half or even less, the salary which men would ask, because the female teacher has only to sustain herself; she does not look forward to the duty of supporting a family, should she marry; nor has she the ambition to amass a fortune, nor is she obliged to give from her earnings support to the State or Government. . . .

7th That most young women who must earn a livelihood can't afford an education.

8th While they get education gratuitously yet these women will teach children at less expense; therefore the whole country is vastly the gainer by this system.

9th That it is not designed to make a class of *celibates,* but that these maiden school teachers will be better prepared to enter the marriage state, after the term of three or four years in their office of instructors, than by any other mode of passing their youth from seventeen or eighteen to twenty-one. That earlier marriages are productive of much of the unhappiness of married women, of many sorrows, sickness, and premature decay and death, there can be no doubt. We look to the development of this system of constituting WOMAN THE EDUCATOR OF THE YOUNG, giving her the fitting requirements, as a measure which will not only preserve her natural gifts and graces of person and character, but enhance them a hundred fold, making her truly what the apostle declares her to be, "the glory of man." [32]

Although the noble congressmen failed to act upon Mrs. Hale's petition, she was undaunted and continued her campaign.[33] Sometimes, as in April 1853, she used the time-honored device of quoting herself. Again she made clear that she did "not design to make a class of *celibates*" but wished to give young ladies the opportunity to teach a few years before marriage.[34]

Mrs. Davis in her letter from Washington in *The Una* in February 1854 commented favorably upon the petition but expressed "surprise at the ignorance of the writer in saying women are not expected

32. *Ibid.,* vol. XLV, no. 2, August 1852, p. 193.
33. *Ibid.,* vol. XLVI, no. 2, February 1853, pp. 176–177; vol. XLVII, no. 7, December 1853, p. 555; vol. LII, January 1856, pp. 82–83.
34. *Ibid.,* vol. XLVI, no. 4, April 1853, p. 370.

to pay from their earnings in support of the state. . . ." [35] Neither
criticism nor lack of action by successive congresses deterred Mrs.
Hale. In January 1856, she again set forth her memorial to Congress, that ". . . THREE OR FOUR MILLIONS OF ACRES OF THE PUBLIC
NATIONAL DOMAINS be set apart to endow one Normal School in every
state for the gratuitous education of female teachers. . . ." [36] Even
the Civil War did not stop her. In January 1864, the petition for
free normal schools for the education of women teachers again
appeared.[37] This is one of the few instances in which Mrs. Hale,
despite her vigor and persistence, was unsuccessful. While the public
domain was not set apart to endow normal schools, by the Morrill
Act of 1862 lands were given to the states and territories to help
establish colleges for teaching agriculture and mechanic arts. Could
a petition in the *Lady's Book* have suggested a means of procedure
to members of Congress?

The ladies' magazines were more successful in presenting other
aspects of teaching. R. G. Chaney in "Thoughts on Teaching" insisted that "every teacher has or ought to have his own mode" of
discipline, and "should pursue the method which experience has
taught him to be the most successful." [38] Advice was given to teachers. In 1840 Mrs. Lydia Sigourney in "Self Educating Teachers" [39]
gave approbation to the "teachers who kept alive within themselves
that habit of constant improvement." [40] Teachers were reminded
of the importance of example.[41] The reviewer of *A Treatise upon
Common School Education, containing Practical Suggestions to
Teachers and Parents* by Charles Northend, A.M., Superintendent
of Public Schools of Danvers, Mass., recommended it, because it
furnished "to parents as well as teachers numerous practical suggestions in regard to their individual and reciprocal duties." [42] Mrs.
Bloomer endorsed the first issue of *Popular Education,* a monthly

35. *The Una,* vol. II, no. 2, February 1854, pp. 218–219 (quotation p. 219).
36. *Godey's Lady's Book,* vol. LII, no. 1, January 1856, pp. 82–83.
37. *Ibid.,* vol. LXVIII, no. 1, January 1864, p. 95.
38. *Ladies' Repository,* vol. XIII, no. 4, April 1853, p. 166.
39. *Godey's Lady's Book,* vol. XX, no. 3, March 1840, pp. 140–142.
40. *Ibid.,* p. 142.   41. *Ibid.,* vol. LI, no. 1, July 1855, p. 83.
42. *Ibid.,* vol. XLVII, no. 4, October 1853, p. 370.

published in New York, for it proposed "to take in the whole scope of useful knowledge, and to furnish an aid to all persons who engage in the work of self-instruction." [43] A writer in the *North American Review* recommended highly *The School and Schoolmaster, a Manual for the Use of Teachers, Employers, Trustees, Inspectors, &c. of Common Schools* by Alonzo Potter, D.D., of New York and George B. Emerson of Massachusetts.[44] Mrs. Swisshelm commended *Popular Education* by Ira Mayew, the late superintendent of public instruction in Michigan, to parents and teachers.[45]

Accounts of teachers' institutes were given.[46] In 1852, Miss Anthony obtained permission to speak in behalf of her sister teachers.[47] In an account of Broome County Teachers Institute in 1859,[48] R. V. Lewis pointed out "the need of women teachers to receive the same pay as men, since it costs as much to educate us [i. e. women] as much to feed and clothe us, as much to doctor us, and as much to bury us, as men; yet for the same labor we receive one-third, or at most one-half the amount paid them. Surely this is not justice and cannot long continue. The light which dawned upon the world in the presentation of the alphabet to women, will not reach its meridian till her wrongs are all righted and humanity stands on equal footing. . . ." [49] These views were unusual. Women teachers accepted or were forced to accept the realistic view so well expressed by Mrs. Hale, that women could afford to teach for lower wages than men.[50] The leadership in most teachers' institutes was given to men, at times to "men of enlarged views, free thought, and good common sense—the latter one of the rarest commodities in society." [51]

The ladies' magazines presented book reviews of books on education, as that of *American Education Its Principles and Elements* by

43. *The Lily,* vol. V, no. 2, June 1, 1853, p. 4.
44. *North American Review,* vol. LVII, no. CXX, July 1843, pp. 149–155.
45. *Pittsburgh Saturday Visiter,* vol. III, no. 48, December 14, 1850, p. 190.
46. *The Lily,* vol. VIII, no. 15, August 1, 1856, p. 107.
47. *The Sibyl,* vol. IV, no. 4, August 15, 1859, p. 607.
48. *Ibid.,* vol. IV, no. 9, November 1, 1859, pp. 647–648.
49. *Ibid.,* p. 648.
50. *Godey's Lady's Book,* vol. XLV, no. 2, August 1852, p. 193.
51. *The Sibyl,* vol. IV, no. 5, September 1, 1859, p. 612.

E. D. Mansfield in *The Ladies' Parlor Companion,*[52] reviews of text-books, as that of the *First Book in Spanish—Practical Introduction to the Study of Spanish* [53] and of *Physiology for Schools* by Reynell Coate, M.D.,[54] in the *Lady's Book* and of the "allegorical novel" of Mrs. Phelps, *Ida Norman,*[55] which the *Southern Quarterly Review* considered "emphatically a work on education." [56] "The Philosophy of Phonetics" was learnedly discussed by Alexander Patobeon in successive issues of the *Lady's Book.*[57] The need for Southern text-books was stressed.[58]

Accounts of the work of European educators were given. The work of an "ingenious German, named Pestalozzi" was described. "Lessons on Objects" were presented in order that it might be understood how the mind of a child could be influenced in other ways than through the printed page.[59] Suggestions were made for study, as on the importance of reading by subjects, and keeping a card index of facts.[60] These more unusual methods of teaching showed the need of trained teachers and the further training of experienced teachers. Teachers' institutes were frequently recommended.[61]

There were penetrating criticisms of teachers and their work. One entitled *The School Library,* strangely enough, gave much food for thought.

52. *Ladies' Parlor Companion, a Collection of Scattered Fragments and Literary Gems,* New York, 142 Nassau Street, 1852, p. 40.

53. *Godey's Lady's Book,* vol. XXXVII, no. 4, October 1847, p. 249.

54. *Ibid.,* vol. XXIV, no. 4, April 1842, p. 239.

55. *Ibid.,* vol. XXXVI, no. 5, May 1848, p. 309.

56. *Southern Quarterly Review,* vol. XIII, no. 26, April 1848, pp. 331–346.

57. *Godey's Lady's Book,* vol. XXXVI, no. 3, March 1848, pp. 170–171; no. 4, April 1848, pp. 225–226; no. 6, June 1848, pp. 347–349.

58. *The Magnolia,* vol. I, (new series) no. 1, July 1842, pp. 59–60; no. 2, August 1842, p. 126; *DeBow's Review and Industrial Resources Statistics, etc.,* vol. XXV, July 1858, pp. 117–118.

59. *The Western Journal of Agriculture, Manufacture, Mechanic Arts, Internal Improvement, Commerce, and General Literature,* vol. III, no. 11, November 1849, pp. 117–129.

60. *The Western Messenger, Devoted to Religion and Literature,* vol. II, no. 1, August 1836, pp. 49–50.

61. *The Western Monthly Magazine,* vol. I, no. 1, January 1833, pp. 10–19; *The Western Journal of Agriculture, Manufacture, Mechanic Arts, Internal Improvement, Commerce, and General Literature,* vol. II, no. 1, January 1849, pp. 34–37.

. . . But in the various departments of the intellectual, the economical tendencies of the age have been most successful. There exists in the most active operation throughout the civilized world, a vast system of thought saving machinery. This is, indeed, a knowing, but not a thinking age. Knowledge is substituted for thought. . . . Book-learning and learning by rote, are supplanting self-communion. The mind is made a store-house, rather than a laboratory. The books that multiply so fast, are mainly products of compilation and dilution. . . . It is no generation of thinkers, we fear, that our popular school systems are training up. . . . Everything is brought up to the last degree of simplification. If, in any existing school-book, it is discovered that room is left for the action of the scholar's mind, a new book comes out at once, expressly to remedy the defect. The wholesome theory that there should be a copartnership of intellect between the writer and the learner is all exploded. The process of instruction is like the decanting of old wine into new bottles; and books are the tunnel. The fancied perfection of teaching consists in making it as much as possible like play. The fundamental maxim of fashionable education is, "The mind is not to be taxed"; and the mind on which no tax is levied, pays none. Mathematics are taught by toys; geography and history must be mixed with equal portions of Peter Parley's mythology; the mysterious differences between active, passive and neuter verbs, instead of being beaten into children's brains, as of old, by hard blows, are most kindly, yet not more wisely illustrated by the picture of a whipping, while all the mooted points in moral philosophy, which have baffled the wisdom of ages, are dispatched in a thin 18 mo., which treats but of tops and of whistles, broken glass and stolen sweet-meats. Even in the study of the ancient languages the good old days of hard work and thoughtful analysis with grammar and dictionary, it is almost deserted; . . . Same thought saving tendency marks the prevailing habit of reading. There exists among all classes of the community, a desire to be deemed or styled *intellectual*. And this sadly abused term is applied rather according to what one reads, than to what one is. . . .[62]

There were, however, articles about teaching which showed a great deal of sympathetic understanding of the teacher.

. . . There are indications of the rise of an order of professional teachers who mean to keep their position from choice, and to carry

62. *North American Review,* vol. L, no. CVII, April 1840, pp. 505–515.

into their work much of the new and better spirit of the age. The
numbers and interests of this order will be greatly promoted by
whatever gives mental and bodily health to the pursuit. That health
does not always attend the profession of teaching is an undoubted
fact, and for obvious reasons. The teacher often unites the sedentary
life with the vexations of business, and is shut up all day like a
student, often, too, in a close atmosphere while his nerves, instead
of being soothed by the still air of delightful studies, are jarred and
irritated by the buzzing of a hundred urchins, and by the chronic
roguery of some dozen of them. He is apt to be too weary to take
active exercise after school, and he finds it hard to be much in the
open air before school hours, the six hours of prescribed school-
house work leaving not much time on his hands after his various tasks
of preparation and review have been attended to. Only a brave
person can meet this difficulty, and secure to him mental and bodily
health by vigorous exercise and genial sociality. . . .[63]

Not only did the ladies' magazines and their literary contemporaries describe and participate in the movement to secure trained
teachers and in that to provide in-service training for teachers, but
some of the writers were frank in exposing what they deemed to be
the defects of contemporary education, while others showed a rare
understanding of the work and the aims of teachers.

63. *Harper's New Monthly Magazine*, vol. XX, no. CXCIII, March 1860,
p. 552 (entire article pp. 550–555 inc.).

CHAPTER EIGHT

The Training of Children

ONE phase of education in which the magazines for ladies showed greater interest than their literary and educational contemporaries was the training of children. In many respects, the ladies' magazines themselves became the educators. In writing, "Woman's highest duty is to guard and guide and instruct her children," [1] Henry F. Harrington was voicing the consensus of opinion of writers in the ladies' magazines.[2] The importance of childhood in the development of the individual was fully appreciated. The editor of *Godey's Lady's Book* noted that Lord Brougham considered the first eighteen months of a child's life the most important, Dr. Babbington, the first nine years, the Roman Catholic Church the first seven years, and then asked pertinently, "Who will establish a school for children's nurses?" [3] She had on numerous occasions indicated that she considered it the duty of mothers to educate their children; they should, if possible, be their children's nurses.[4] Her query pointed to the need for the education of women as an aspect of the training of children.

1. *Ladies' Companion*, vol. IX, no. 8, October 1838, pp. 293–296 (quotation p. 294).
2. Similar statements were made: *Godey's Lady's Book*, vol. XXX, no. 3, March 1845, p. 108; *Graham's Illustrated Magazine of Literature, Romance, Art, and Fashion*, vol. LIII, no. 3, September 1858, pp. 245–249, especially p. 245; *Ladies' Magazine*, vol. II, no. VII, July 1829, pp. 317–319; *Ladies' Repository*, vol. XIV, no. 10, October 1854, pp. 433–436, "Mothers and the Destiny of Their Children" by the editor, showed how Cowper, Napoleon, Lord Brougham, Schiller and Southey were so influenced; *Southern Lady's Companion*, vol. II, no. 11, February 1849, pp. 249–250, "The Profession of Women," by Miss C. R. Beecher; *Ibid.*, vol. V, no. 5, August 1851, pp. 121–124, "Women in the Relation of Mother," by Bishop Andrew.
3. *Godey's Lady's Book*, vol. L, no. 2, February 1855, p. 175.
4. *Ibid.*, vol. XXX, no. 3, March 1845, p. 108.

When unfortunately, it was impossible for mothers because of employment to care for their children, Mrs. Hale, early in her editorial career, suggested that the children be sent to Infant Schools.[5] The first Infant School had been established in 1815 by Robert Owen at New Lanark, Scotland. There the children were "trained in habits of order and cleanliness, to abstain from quarrels, to be kind to each other." [6] Subsequently through the efforts of Samuel Wilderspin, similar infant schools, where children under seven were taught reading, arithmetic, a little geography and natural history as well as the facts of the New Testament, were opened in England.

By 1830 infant schools had been established in Boston, New York and Philadelphia.[7] Mrs. Sarah Josepha Hale in her *Ladies' Magazine* kept her readers informed of their progress. She described the Bedford Street School for Infants in Boston; [8] noted the establishment of the Salem Street School, the one on Stillman Street and the African Infant School on Belknap Street, Boston; [9] endorsed Dr. Beecher's plea in his church for the support of infant schools;[10] commended the pioneer work of Miss Eliza Riply of Boston in establishing an infant school, eighteen miles from Nashville, Tennessee; [11] rejoiced in the progress of infant schools in New York, where they were supported at public expense and in Philadelphia, where charitable bequests for them had been made; [12] urged New England to make her system of public schools complete by seeing that primary schools

5. *Ladies' Magazine,* vol. II, no. VI, June 1829, p. 291; *Ibid.,* vol. II, no. VII, July 1829, pp. 338–339; *American Ladies' Magazine,* vol. V, no. III, March 1832, p. 136; *Ibid.,* vol. V, no. IV, April 1832, pp. 179–182.
6. Quoted in Noble, *op. cit.,* p. 203.
7. *Ibid.,* pp. 202–204; Ellwood H. Cubberley, *Public Education in the United States* (Boston, Houghton Mifflin Company, 1919, pp. xxv, 517) pp. 96–100; Reisner, *op. cit.,* pp. 257–260.
8. *Ladies' Magazine,* vol. II, no. VI, June 1829, p. 291; vol. II, no. VII, July 1829, pp. 338–339.
9. *American Ladies' Magazine,* vol. V, no. IV, April 1832, pp. 172–182.
10. *Ibid.,* vol. V, no. III, March 1832, p. 136.
11. *Ibid.,* vol. VI, no. XII, December 1833, pp. 562–564; vol. VIII, no. IX, September 1835, pp. 504–506 (a letter of description); vol. VIII, no. X, October 1835, pp. 575–577 (letter from Miss Riply).
12. *Ibid.,* vol. V, no. IV, April 1832, p. 181.

were "preceded by a system of instruction either in the nursery or in the schools"; [13] and printed much of the Seventh Annual Report of the Infant School Society of the City of Boston.[14] Mrs. Caroline Gillman in her *Southern Rose Bud* told of an excellent infant school in Charleston, South Carolina, where the average daily attendance was from thirty to forty children.[15]

Mrs. Hale even recommended that infant schools should not be confined to the children of the poor, for not only did they relieve a mother of her charge, but more important, they provided better facilities for the teaching of the "little ones." [16] Later, however, she stated that she had "never urged their adoption, by those who have means to provide for their infants and time to take care of them." [17]

The aim of both Mrs. Hale [18] and Mrs. Gilman [19] in bringing infant schools to the attention of their readers was to secure funds. As Mrs. Hale pointedly put it, "they must depend chiefly on the efforts of the ladies." [20]

Mrs. Gilman contented herself with calling the infant school in Charleston excellent; [21] but Mrs. Hale noted desirable features. She insisted that schools should be housed in a convenient room and "faithful and discreet agents employed." [22] She rejoiced that the children were instructed "in those things which pertain to life that now is and that which is to come." [23] She described several schools. In the Atkinson Street School (formerly Salem Street) in Boston about seventy children between the ages of one and four were housed in

13. *Ibid.*, p. 182. The same idea is found in *Ladies' Magazine,* vol. II, no. VI, June 1829, p. 291.

14. *American Ladies' Magazine,* vol. VIII, no. V, May 1835, pp. 293–294.

15. *Southern Rose Bud,* vol. 2, no. 50, August 9, 1834, p. 199.

16. *Ladies' Magazine,* vol. II, no. II, February 1829, p. 89; vol. II, no. VI, June 1829, p. 291.

17. *American Ladies' Magazine,* vol. V, no. VI, April 1832, p. 180.

18. *Ibid.*, vol. V, no. III, March 1832, p. 136; vol. V, no. IV, April 1832, pp. 179–182.

19. *Southern Rose Bud,* vol. 2, no. 50, August 9, 1834, p. 199.

20. *Ladies' Magazine,* vol. II, no. VI, June 1829, p. 291.

21. *Southern Rose Bud,* vol. 2, no. 50, August 9, 1834, p. 199.

22. *Ladies' Magazine,* vol. II, no. II, February 1829, p. 89.

23. *American Ladies' Magazine,* vol. V, no. IV, April 1832, p. 180.

two rooms and provided with a yard in which to play. Evidently the
teacher was most successful, for "the little ones seemed happy, indeed almost too merry—more like a nursery than a school." [24] One
hundred seventy "scholars" were registered at the Bedford Street
School but only sixty to ninety attended. Mrs. Hale found their
progress in "knowledge" astonishing and delighted in the admirable
"order" exhibited in the school. Singing was helpful in maintaining
this order, for "whenever any symptom of weariness or inattention
appear[ed] their indefatigable instructress [had] only to strike
the note of one of their simple songs, and instantly the little band
[were] in full and joyous chorus, every eye brighten[ed] every face
[was] cheerful." [25] Mrs. Hale understandingly commented, "The
art of teaching these little ones consists principally in employing that
restlessness, which childhood always displays and which is usually
exercised to do mischief on objects." [26] She realized that even the
best children had "hours of uneasiness," frequently the result of
idleness. Infant schools made children happy by keeping them employed.[27]

To those critics who feared that children would lose their love
for their mothers if they were made happy by strangers, Mrs. Hale
countered with the comment, "If they have been happy at school,
how joyful must they be to prattle of that happiness at home." [28]
She was discursive in answering the criticism of the lack of formal
discipline:

. . . We are aware that objections have been urged against the
discipline of the schools, and the habits of the pupils formed thereby.
It is said that the scholars from the Infant Schools accustomed to the
variety of active exercises and lively recitations are often found
troublesome or discontented when transferred to the primary schools.
The regular order and constant study which these last think it necessary to maintain, seem irksome to a child who has thought marching
and singing and many other pleasant things were connected with the
name of school. Without attempting at this time, to show that the
primary schools would probably be improved by a more liberal and

24. *Ladies' Magazine,* vol. II, no. VII, July 1829, p. 338.
25. *Ibid.,* pp. 338–339.   26. *Ibid.,* p. 338.
27. *Ibid.,* vol. II, no. II, February 1829, p. 89.   28. *Ibid.*

familiar mode of management, we will observe that faults which may easily be remedied are no good reason for abandoning the system of Infant Schools, when their necessity to the very poor is so apparent. . . ." [29]

Like Mrs. Hale, educators saw possibilities for improving primary schools through a more liberal and familiar mode of management. Infant schools by their adaptation of method to the age of the children contributed very greatly to the development of primary schools.[30]

After the middle 1830's, however, infant schools dropped from the attention of Mrs. Hale and other editors. In 1854, a writer in *The Builder* described a nursery for infants, where children with "bleached countenances" were left by parents who were obliged to work. There, "on payment of a small sum," the children were "well cared for, in a clean and well ventilated place, lodged in snug little beds and supplied with playthings, and the best of instruction for early years kind and pleasant words." [31] This was a nursery rather than an infant school. It indicated interest in the care rather than the education of little children.

This interest in the care of little children, shown by many editors of ladies' magazines, was not shared by the writers in educational journals who were inclined to confine their attention to children at school. In a German periodical, however, there was an account in 1860 of the development of the Kindergarten by Froebel.[32] Here again the care and the education of the child were united; but this German development was not described before the Civil War in the publications in English.

To most of the editors of ladies' magazines then the best place for the education of little children was in the home under the direction of the mother. In these mid-nineteenth century ladies' magazines

29. *American Ladies' Magazine,* vol. V, no. IV, April 1832, p. 180.

30. Noble, *op. cit.,* pp. 202–205; Reisner, *op. cit.,* pp. 257–260; Cubberley, *op. cit.,* pp. 96–100.

31. Quoted in *Home Journal,* whole no. 442, series for 1854, no. 31, July 29, 1854, p. 4.

32. *Blätter für Freies Religiöses Leben,* 4ter Jahrg. no. 10, April 1860, pp. 149–153.

there was an almost complete lack of emphasis on the physical care of children. Food for children was seldom mentioned. It was taken for granted that a mother would nurse her baby or secure a wet nurse for it. Dr. Jno. Stainback Wilson in 1860 in *Godey's Lady's Book* pointed out that the diet of nursing women should be chiefly vegetables, with meat once or at most twice a day and that no stimulants as tea, coffee, wine, or cordials should be used.[33] On one occasion the fashion editor of the *Lady's Book* noted that when the infant, clad in its best "walking dress" was carried in the arms of its nurse to visit its "expectant aunts and grandmothers," each would give it a luncheon of "barley sugar." The "barley sugar" was incidental; the writer was intent on describing the "walking dress," which at a hundred dollars, she considered "far too expensive."[34] No mother could have perused any of the fashion magazines and been unaware of what the well-dressed infant, little boy and little girl, should wear. The emphasis was on showing fashions and only occasionally on making garments. Food was treated in a similar way; "receipts" were indefinite and before the days of calories and vitamines, science seems to have played no part in the feeding of growing children. Of the importance of training them in desirable habits, the writers of a century ago seem almost unaware and then only in relation to their living a righteous life.[35]

Rather was the stress placed almost exclusively upon molding a child's character. Because of the emphasis on ethical training as preparation for life hereafter, the editors usually stated basic principles which they thought parents, especially mothers, should follow. The Biblical injunction "Train up a child on the way he should go, and when he is old he will not depart from it" formed the basis of the advice of ministerial editors and pious laity [36] alike. Parents were reminded that "oaks are rooted by the tempests" and that children should be "trained to meet the vicissitudes of life." [37] One lone clergyman felt that a child should be taught primarily to "avoid

33. *Godey's Lady's Book,* vol. LXI, no. 6, December 1860, p. 558.
34. *Ibid.,* vol. XLVI, no. 4, April 1853, p. 381.
35. *Friend of Virtue,* vol. XI, no. 23, December 1848, p. 362–363 (editorial).
36. *The Lily,* vol. I, no. 2, February 1, 1849, p. 12 (editorial).
37. *South-Western Monthly,* vol. I, no. I, January 1852, pp. 16–18.

intemperance and licentiousness."[38] For the most part editors believed that the relationship between the child and God should be the basis of training.[39] The child should be led "to see God's providence in most of the striking phenomenon of natural science."[40] He should be taught to respect His will by submitting to duty.[41] He should learn to fear and to love God.[42]

The child should not only learn to love God but he should learn to love his fellow-men. Suggestions of ways to help her child to cultivate this love were made to mothers. When a new baby arrived she should help her child understand that he and the baby were not rivals.[43] As she watched him in his play she should check his selfishness by teaching him "liberality and benevolence" and by showing him "that it is noble, generous and praiseworthy to minister to the wants and the comforts of others."[44] He should be taught not to fight; even as a little boy he should learn that he must not hit his younger brother.[45] In 1830, Catharine Beecher had pointed out that the world was no longer governed by physical force but by the influence mind exerts over mind and suggested that this dictum be the basis of education in the home as well as school.[46]

There was agreement among the advisers of mothers that children should be ruled by the forces of justice, reason,[47] kindness and love.[48]

38. *Advocate of Moral Reform*, vol. VII, no. 7, April 1841, p. 50.

39. "Religious Ideas the Basis of Education" by Rev. Edward Thompson, D.D. in *Ladies' Repository*, vol. XIV, no. 4, April 1854, pp. 145–149; no. 5, May 1854, pp. 224–227; "My Aunt's Advice about Bringing up Children" in *Ladies' Repository*, vol. XIV, no. 11, November 1854, pp. 482–486.

40. Quoted from *Quarterly Review* in *Godey's Lady's Book*, vol. XLVI, March 1853, p. 213.

41. *American Ladies' Magazine*, vol. VIII, no. 6, June 1835, pp. 335–339, especially p. 335.

42. *Southern Lady's Companion*, vol. III, no. 12, March 1850, pp. 266–267, especially p. 267.

43. *Frank Leslie's Magazine*, vol. III, no. 4, October 1858, p. 344.

44. *Southern Lady's Companion*, vol. III, no. 1, April 1849, pp. 3–4.

45. *The Una*, vol. II, no. 11, November 1854, p. 367. Based on a quotation from Elihu Burritt "I Mustn't Hit Little Harry."

46. *Ladies' Miscellany*, vol. II, no. 20, August 18, 1830, p. 78.

47. *Godey's Lady's Book*, vol. XXXI, no. 6, December 1845, p. 269.

48. *Ibid.*, vol. XLII, no. 1, January 1851, pp. 47–50, especially p. 48, letter of Louis Gaylord Clark to the editor.

Under no circumstances should they experience bodily fear, "a debasing and demoralizing influence." [49] One editor, Mrs. Swisshelm, even went so far as to insist that all corporal punishment be prohibited by law.[50]

Another principle upon which there was conformity of opinion was that a child should understand the principles by which he was governed.[51] Only in this way could he develop self-respect, self-control,[52] and self-government.[53] Children should learn to be honest,[54] to obey,[55] and to accept the decision of parents in the case of a dispute.[56] They should be taught not to swear.[57] Parents in their turn should treat children like human-beings.[58] They should be kind [59] and patient [60] and should not scold [61] or find fault with them but encourage them.[62] They should see that their children have a happy childhood [63] and remember that in training, example is more important than precept.[64]

49. *Ibid.,* vol. XXVIII, no. 2, February 1844, pp. 80–83, especially p. 82; also same idea in *Southern Lady's Companion,* vol. 5, no. 2, May 1851, pp. 51–52.

50. *Pittsburgh Saturday Visiter,* vol. IV, no. XLVIII, December 20, 1851, p. 190.

51. *Southern Lady's Companion,* vol. II, no. 12, March 1849, pp. 271–272; *Godey's Lady's Book,* vol. XXI, no. 6, December 1840, p. 274.

52. *Godey's Lady's Book,* vol. XXVIII, no. 2, February 1844, pp. 80–83, "The Rights of Children," by Mrs. Emma C. Embury.

53. *American Ladies' Magazine,* vol. VIII, no. XI, November 1835, pp. 597–604.

54. *Godey's Lady's Book,* vol. XLVI, no. 2, February 1853, p. 178.

55. *Advocate of Moral Reform,* vol. VII, no. 7, April 1, 1841, p. 50, quoted from *American Citizen; Godey's Lady's Book,* vol. LV, no. 4, October 1857, pp. 344–345.

56. *Friend of Virtue,* vol. XI, no. 17, September 1, 1848, pp. 275–277.

57. *Ibid.,* vol. XI, no. 14, July 15, 1848, pp. 215–216.

58. *Godey's Lady's Book,* vol. XXXI, December 1845, p. 269.

59. *Ibid.,* vol. XLII, January 1851, pp. 47–50.

60. *Ibid.,* vol. LVIII, April 1859, pp. 336–337.

61. *American Ladies' Magazine,* vol. VIII, no. 6, June 1835, p. 339; *Advocate of Moral Reform,* vol. VII, no. 5, March 1, 1841, pp. 36–37, and no. 6, March 15, 1841, p. 41, quoted from *Female Advocate* of London.

62. *Godey's Lady's Book,* vol. LIX, no. 6, December 1859, p. 555.

63. *Ibid.,* vol. LX, no. 3, March 1860, pp. 272–274.

64. *Ibid.,* vol. LI, no. 1, July 1855, p. 83; *Southern Lady's Companion,* vol. II, no. 6, September 1848, p. 142.

To the mother who accepted the principles but did not know how to translate them into action, Mrs. Hale recommended that she "study, not books or rules so much as the temperament and disposition of her children, and the effects which her treatment and the circumstances that surround her and them produce day by day on their feelings and characters." [65] There were specific suggestions. A mother should keep her sons off the street and in the house in the evening; she should take an interest in their enjoyment, try to help them cultivate a fondness for reading,[66] and encourage them to experiment.[67] She should see that her children had an opportunity to read the Bible and urge them to do so.[68] She should keep them from bad company.[69]

Parents were thus instructed in the care of their children. The instruction reflects the theological teachings of the nineteenth century rather than the ideas of educators. Infant schools which were sponsored in the 1830's by Mrs. Hale and Mrs. Gilman were subsequently incorporated into the elementary schools—and the kindergarten described in a German magazine in 1860 has since become part of the public school system. Thus the ladies' magazines participated in the development of elementary education and were themselves an important means of educating parents.

65. *Godey's Lady's Book,* vol. XXIII, July 1841, pp. 41–42.
66. *Advocate of Moral Reform,* vol. VII, no. 17, September 1, 1841, pp. 131–132, "On Management of Boys," by Rev. J. S. C. Abbott.
67. *Godey's Lady's Book,* vol. LV, no. 4, October 1857, pp. 344–345.
68. *Ibid.,* vol. LVII, no. 2, August 1858, p. 179; *Friend of Virtue,* vol. XI, no. 23, December 1848, pp. 362–363.
69. *Advocate of Moral Reform,* vol. VII, no. 10, May 1, 1841, p. 71.

CHAPTER NINE

Education of the Handicapped

A<small>T</small> times editors of both ladies' magazines and popular periodicals, looked upon educational activities as "news." Such was their attitude toward the education of the handicapped. Until the nineteenth century, the handicapped had been looked upon by most of the civilized world as social outcasts to be endured rather than helped. There had been isolated cases of the education of the blind and deaf.

The blind, especially, had aroused human sympathy which unleashed the intelligence of a few to work on the problem of the individual blind person. It was not until 1785, however, that Valentin Haüy, encouraged by the success of his pupil, founded in Paris the first school for the blind. He taught his students to read by means of raised letters. So successful was he that his school was supported first by private subscription and then by state funds. In many respects this school has been both the model and the inspiration of those for the blind all over the world. Dr. John D. Fisher, a young American physician, who had visited it, was instrumental in founding in 1829 the Perkins Institute of the Blind at Boston. T. H. Perkins gave his mansion to house the school; the state contributed financial support. This combination of private philanthropy and public aid is typical of most of the schools for the blind in the days before the Civil War. These institutions were often known as asylums or homes. Workshops were usually connected with them. By 1844, such schools had been established at New York, Philadelphia, Columbus, Staunton, Louisville and Nashville. Largely through the talent of Dr. Samuel G. Howe, the director of the Perkins Institute for nearly forty-four years, and through the prowess of his most noteworthy pupil, the blind deaf-mute, Laura

Bridgman, the Institute maintained a unique leadership in this field.

The education of the deaf in the United States came about in much the same way as that for the blind. In 1815, Dr. Thomas Hopkins Gallaudet was sent abroad by a group of citizens of Hartford, Connecticut, to study the methods of teaching the deaf. On his return, he became, in 1816, the director of the newly established Connecticut Asylum at Hartford. Similar institutions were established in Pennsylvania, New York, and Kentucky. In some respects the one at Hartford was the pattern for the Perkins Institute as well as for most of the schools for the deaf. At Hartford, Dr. Howe saw the achievement of Julia Brace, another blind deaf-mute. He later stated that some of the ideas he used in teaching Laura Bridgman had been suggested by the work done with Julia Brace. The prowess of Julia Brace and Laura Bridgman was the subject of articles in magazines for ladies,[1] as well as in educational journals.[2] The wonder of the achievement of the two girls was stressed in the popular periodicals. They recounted what the girls could do. In commenting upon Dr. Howe's report of Laura's progress, the *National Anti-Slavery Standard* pertinently remarked ". . . we trust that the Legislature in their zeal for economy will not withhold their customary aid . . ."[3]

1. About Julia Brace—*Southern Rose Bud,* vol. II, no. 40, May 31, 1834, pp. 157–158; about Laura Bridgman—*National Anti-Slavery Standard,* vol. I, no. 45, April 15, 1841, p. 180; vol. VII, no. 1, whole no. 313, June 4, 1846, p. 4; *North American Review,* vol. LII, no. 4, April 1841, pp. 467–468; *Pittsburgh Saturday Visiter,* vol. III, no. 48, December 14, 1850, p. 193; *Universalist and Ladies' Repository,* vol. IX, no. 2, July 1840, pp. 50–51.

2. *American Journal of Education,* vol. X, December 1857, pp. 383–400 (by S. G. Howe, M.D.); *Common School Journal,* vol. II, no. 6, March 16, 1840, pp. 91–96; vol. III, no. 3, February 1, 1841, pp. 33 ff. (entire issue); no. 4, February 15, 1841, pp. 49–51; vol. IV, no. 10, May 16, 1842, pp. 145–160 (entire issue); no. 11, June 1, 1842, pp. 161–162; vol. VII, no. 10, May 15, 1845, pp. 145–160 (entire issue); no. 11, June 2, 1845, pp. 161–166; vol. V, no. 10, May 15, 1843, pp. 145–159; no. 11, June 1, 1843, pp. 161–166; *The Common School Journal of the State of Pennsylvania,* vol. I, no. 1, January 15, 1844, pp. 16–22; no. 2, February 15, 1844, pp. 56–64; no. 4, April 15, 1844, pp. 108–114; no. 6, June 15, 1844, pp. 186–190; no. 7, July 15, 1844, pp. 218–244; no. 8, August 15, 1844, pp. 249–256; no. 10, October 15, 1844, pp. 314–320; no. 11, November 15, 1844, pp. 348–352.

3. *National Anti-Slavery Standard,* vol. I, no. 45, April 15, 1841, p. 180.

The comments in the educational journals were equally pertinent. Horace Mann quoted Dr. Howe's Reports at length in the *Common School Journal*. These he usually introduced with a significant note.

. . . If science and skill in a teacher can do so much to develop the powers of the mind, without the aid of the senses, what cannot science and skill do with their aid?

If a child, who is deprived of the senses, learns so much and behaves so well, what ought those children to learn and to do, whom God has blessed with the means of knowledge and of doing good.[4]

The history of Laura Bridgman throws so much *light* on the whole subject of education, that we propose to continue in this number of the Journal the accounts of that remarkable child. . . . [The teacher] will see how much progress can be made with any pupil, if he begins rightly and teaches thoroughly. . . .[5]

The comments of John S. Hart in *The Common School Journal of the State of Pennsylvania* were equally pointed.

. . . The case of this unfortunate girl is not only interesting to general readers, but of peculiar interest and importance to those who, as parents, school directors, or teachers are studying the great science of Education. . . .[6]

The educational significance of the work of Gallaudet was noted by Henry Barnard in "Educational Biography, Thomas Hopkins Gallaudet." [7]

Writers in the popular periodicals did not indicate the importance of the work among the blind and the deaf in the development of the science of education. They did, however, suggest to their readers a desirable attitude to take toward the physically handicapped. A deaf and dumb pupil urged that the deaf be aided and instructed, not pitied.[8] Another asked that the deaf and dumb be sent to school.[9]

4. *Common School Journal,* vol. II, no. 6, March 16, 1840, p. 91.

5. *Ibid.,* vol. IV, no. 10, May 16, 1842, pp. 145–146.

6. *The Common School Journal of the State of Pennsylvania,* vol. I, no. 1, January 15, 1844, p. 16.

7. *American Journal of Education,* vol. I, no. IV, May 1856, pp. 417–432. See also: *Ibid.,* pp. 441–446, 443–449.

8. *Home Journal,* whole no. 384, series for 1853, no. 25, June 18, 1853, p. 1.

9. *Godey's Lady's Book,* vol. XXXVI, no. 2, February 1848, pp. 121–122.

Harriet Martineau's letter to the deaf was reprinted. In it, she urged the deaf to be cheerful and matter of fact in accepting their defect, and in no way to ostracize themselves from human companionship. She recounted ways in which she had accepted and urged others to accept the handicap of deafness.[10]

Accounts of work among the blind and the deaf were given. The Blind Asylum of Boston [11] and the School for the Blind on Ninth Avenue, New York [12] were described. Statements about the New York Institute for the Instruction of the Deaf [13] and the Report of the Pennsylvania Institute for the Deaf and the Dumb,[14] the Hartford School for the Deaf [15] and information about the state asylums for the physically handicapped in Michigan and Missouri [16] showed their increasing usefulness. Sometimes the articles were of a technical nature. The work of Haüy, the first to educate the blind scientifically, was discussed.[17] The method of instructing the deaf formed the basis of an article in Russell's *American Journal of Education;* [18] that of instructing the blind the basis of an article in Barnard's *American Journal of Education.*[19] "Education of the Deaf and Dumb in Europe and America" included an historical account, statistics on the deaf, dumb, and blind, and an analysis of the causes of deafness in their relation to heredity and marriage.[20] In the treatment

10. *Southern Rose,* vol. 3, no. 16, April 4, 1835, pp. 121–126.

11. *American Ladies' Magazine,* vol. IX, no. VII, July 1836, p. 410; *Pittsburgh Saturday Visiter,* vol. III, no. 48, December 1850, p. 192; *Gleason's Pictorial Drawing Room Companion,* vol. III, no. 4, July 24, 1852, p. 61.

12. *Ladies' Companion,* vol. IV, no. 12, December 1835, pp. 89–91; *Frank Leslie's Illustrated Newspaper,* vol. I, April 24, 1856, pp. 316–318.

13. *American Journal of Education,* vol. III, no. IX, June 1857, pp. 347–365; *Home Journal,* whole no. 59, series of 1847, no. 13, March 27, p. 2 (not numbered).

14. *Godey's Lady's Book,* vol. LII, no. 5, May 1856, p. 468.

15. *The American Review, a Whig Journal of Politics, Literature, Arts and Science,* vol. III, no. V, May 1846, pp. 497–516.

16. *American Journal of Education,* vol. I, no. 4, May 1856, pp. 447–448.

17. *Ladies' Companion,* vol. IV, no. 2, December 1835, pp. 89–91.

18. *American Journal of Education,* vol. II, no. XI, November 1827, pp. 641–648.

19. *American Journal of Education,* vol. IV, no. X, September 1857, pp. 127–139.

20. *DeBow's Review and Industrial Resources, Statistics, etc.,* vol. XVII, no. 5, December 1854, pp. 435–451.

of the blind and the deaf, as reflected in magazines, is much that is humane and scientific.

The first half of the nineteenth century marked a similar change in the attitude toward the mentally handicapped. Scientific knowledge about them was in its infancy. Yet, even a century ago, writers urged that the feeble-minded and insane be separated; [21] the feeble-minded be educated; [22] the insane, hospitalized. [23] Schools for idiots —the writers used the term as synonymous with feeble-minded— were described, as the Idiot School in Pennsylvania, [24] the one at Barre, Massachusetts, [25] and Mr. Richards' School for Feeble-minded Children in Massachusetts. [26] Accounts of the education of idiots in France, Switzerland, Great Britain and the German towns were given. [27] Cures for idiocy and cretenism were discussed. [28]

The same spirit of humanity was apparent in the attitude toward the criminal in the work of such a leader as Dorothea Dix and in the periodical literature. Two aspects of education with relation to crime were stressed. First, it was believed that there should be definite religious and moral instruction in all prisons, [29] that prisoners should be read to and that women prisoners should be instructed in needlework, knitting and other suitable employments. [30] Second, it was felt that education was a means of preventing crime. Writers in the mid-nineteenth century accepted the premise that all education was training for desirable citizenship and, in a sense, crime prevention. They wrote at length on the judicious use of punishment for children. Throughout the discussions, emphasis was placed

21. *Southern Literary Messenger,* vol. XV, no. 2, February 1849, pp. 65–68.
22. *Ibid.,* p. 68.
23. *Godey's Lady's Book,* vol. XLVIII, no. 6, June 1854, pp. 555–556.
24. *The Una,* vol. II, no. 4, April 1854, p. 255.
25. *Pittsburgh Saturday Visiter,* vol. IV, no. XV, May 3, 1851, p. 59.
26. *National Anti-Slavery Standard,* vol. XIX, no. 19, September 25, 1858, p. 2.
27. *National Anti-Slavery Standard,* vol. VII, no. 38, whole no. 402, February 17, 1848, p. 152; and *Pennsylvania Journal of Prison Discipline and Philanthropy,* vol. IV, no. 1, January 1849, pp. 40–41.
28. *Godey's Lady's Book,* vol LI, no. 6, December 1855, p. 511.
29. *Pennsylvania Journal of Prison Discipline and Philanthropy,* vol. I, no. I, January 1845, pp. 77–81.
30. *Ibid.,* vol. I, no. 2, April 1845, p. 97.

on the development of the character of the individual.[31] "Evening School, for the benefit of working classes," [32] the Y.M.C.A., and "City Missionaries to visit the poor" [33] were means of reform and of crime prevention.

In a country where Negro slavery prevailed, Negroes, whether free or slave, were socially and educationally handicapped. With respect to the education of the slaves, a writer in *DeBow's Review* stated definitely "that the State is *not* required to provide education for the great bulk of its laboring class." [34] Slaves were at times taught in a plantation school. Even in the North, custom and popular opinion often decreed that Negroes be educated in schools supported by private philanthropy rather than by public funds. In Washington the right of private philanthropy to educate Negroes was challenged. Miss Miner's School for Negro and Mulatto girls there was attacked by "His Majesty King Mob"; but it was later unmolested, because "Mrs. President Pierce," when she heard that a "riotous suppression was imminent, drove repeatedly in her carriage to inquire into the progress of the school and be assured of its prospects and safety." [35] Nearly two decades earlier, opposition to Miss Crandall's School for Females of Color at Canterbury, Connecticut, had served "only to bring the institution more into notice." [36] The Friends were interested in the "instruction of adult colored persons." [37] An African Educational Society was formed to teach colored persons in order to qualify them for usefulness and influence in

31. *Common School Journal of the State of Pennsylvania*, vol. I, no. 12, December 15, 1844, pp. 364–365; *DeBow's Review and Industrial Resources, Statistics, etc.*, vol. XVIII, o.s., vol. I, n.s., no. III, March 1855, pp. 409–421; *Pittsburgh Saturday Visiter*, vol. II, no. 21, May 26, 1849, p. 76. See Chapter Eight of this study.

32. *Godey's Lady's Book* vol. L, no. 3, March 1855, p. 271; *Pittsburgh Saturday Visiter*, vol. IV, no. XLI, January 10, 1852, p. 202.

33. *Godey's Lady's Book*, vol. L, no. 3, March 1855, p. 271.

34. *DeBow's Review and Industrial Resources, Statistics, etc.*, vol. XX, second series vol. X, February 1856, pp. 143–156 (quotation p. 148).

35. *National Anti-Slavery Standard*, vol. XVII, no. 52, May 16, 1857, p. 1 (whole no. 884). Other accounts: *Ibid.*, vol. XVIII, no. 30, whole no. 914, December 12, 1857, p. 3; *The Una*, vol. III, no. 4, April 1855, p. 57.

36. *American Annals of Education*, vol. III, no. VI, June 1833, p. 287.

37. *Ibid.*, p. 284.

Africa.[38] An appeal was made for the support of a colored orphan asylum, where children from two to eight were "thoroughly grounded in the rudiments of practical education." [39] The excellent work of the Cincinnati High School, established in 1844, by H. S. Gilmore for the benefit of colored children from the ages of six to twenty, had "wrought a very great change in that class of the population." [40] Several editors were aware of the desirability of the education of Negroes.

While editors varied in their interests, there were always some who were interested in securing educational opportunities for those who were physically, mentally or socially handicapped. It was felt that through education the lot of all would be improved. The physically handicapped would become happy and independent. Mental inequalities would be eradicated and corrected. Crime would be eliminated. The Negro would become the equal of the white.

38. *American Annals of Education and Instruction and Journal of Literary Institutions, being a continuation of the American Journal of Education,* vol. I, no. 1, January 1831, p. 38.

39. *National Anti-Slavery Standard,* vol. VIII, no. 25, whole no. 389, November 18, 1847, p. 99.

40. *Ibid.,* vol. VI, no. 36, February 5, 1846, whole no. 296, p. 141.

CHAPTER TEN

Medical Education of Women

I<small>N</small> one kind of education, the medical education of women, women editors alone were interested. Educators, for the most part, ignored it. They may in fact not have considered it an educational movement, but an attempt of woman to extend her sphere. Yet, from the historical point of view, the coming of the woman physician marked not the entrance of woman into a new field of labor but her return to one from which she had been excluded. In Colonial America, Western Europe, and among the ancient peoples, women were expected to serve as midwives and to attend the sick. They secured their little training in an apprenticeship system. In fact until well into the nineteenth century in Europe and in America this kind of medical training prevailed for men as well as women. By 1830, however, the graduates of American medical schools, such as those at Pennsylvania and Harvard, and of those famous European medical centers, as Edinburgh, Paris, and Vienna, were the recognized leaders in the medical profession. Consequently these physicians received popular support. Homeopathy and hydropathy also gained a following in the decades before the Civil War. Finally purveyors of patent medicines and quacks siphoned off the credulous from the clientele of the apprentice-trained physician. Medical schools, therefore, grew in number and in enrollment. But they did not admit women.

Elizabeth Blackwell, the first American woman to be graduated from a medical college, had been refused admission by several before she entered the one at Geneva, New York, in the fall of 1847. She gained practical experience during her vacation at the Blockley Almshouse in Philadelphia. After her graduation in the spring of 1849, she continued her study at La Maternité in Paris and St.

Bartholomew's Hospital in London. When she returned to New
York in July of 1851 to begin her practice, two struggling female
medical colleges were offering medical education to women.

Liberal minded men physicians in Boston and Philadelphia had
brought into being these female medical colleges. They had not done
this without the help of the ladies.[1] The Female Medical Education
Society was organized in Boston with this end in view. The Ladies'
Medical Missionary Society of Philadelphia desired to help women
to qualify as physicians in order that they might become medical
missionaries. Mrs. Sarah Josepha Hale was secretary of the latter
organization.[2]

One phase of the medical education of women which greatly dis-
tressed Mrs. Hale was the use of the word "female." In August 1857,
she wrote a lengthy editorial:

Grammatical Errors . . . that the word *female* as now too often
found in our newspapers and popular literature is vulgar and a
blemish in style can be easily tested. . . . We do not say *female
emperor* instead of *empress*. . . . How absurd then to fancy that
female physician elevates woman above the style of *doctress!* The
latter is a pleasant soft word, explaining the rank and sex, mingling
in an idea of the woman and her vocation, tenderness with respect.
The former title is expressed by two words, one meaning an animal,
the other a man, making a compound idea, repulsive, we believe to
almost every ear and injuring the popularity of woman's medical
education and practice. . . .[3]

As in the name "doctress" the editor of the *Lady's Book* saw the
"mingling of an idea of the woman and her vocation," so in the profession of medicine, she saw an extension of woman's "sphere." [4]
Mrs. Davis of *The Una* recognized this same extension, but, in addition, felt that woman had the right as any human being, to be educated in medicine.[5] While the women editors,—Mrs. Hale and Mrs.

1. Cole, *op. cit.,* pp. 176, 184–187; Fish, *op. cit.,* pp. 209–210; Woody, *op. cit.,*
vol. II, pp. 340–362.
2. *Godey's Lady's Book,* vol. XLIV, no. 3, March 1852, pp. 185–188.
3. *Ibid.,* vol. LV, no. 2, August 1857, p. 177 (article—pp. 177–178).
4. *Ibid.,* vol. XLIV, no. 3, March 1852, p. 228.
5. *The Una,* vol. II, no. 11, November 1854, pp. 360–362.

Davis, Mrs. Swisshelm, Mrs. Bloomer and Drs. Hasbrouck approached the right of woman to practice medicine from different philosophical points of view, they jointly waged verbal war on behalf of the woman physician. This war was waged simultaneously and intermittently on three fronts. It was necessary first to establish woman's right to be a physician, second to provide a place for her to receive a medical education, and third to help individual girls and women secure such an education in medical schools and hospitals.

In order to prove her right to a medical education, the editors assembled evidence. It was God's way; "the Bible recognizes and approves *only woman* in the sacred office of *midwife*." Women medical missionaries would be permitted "to carry to the poor suffering women of heathendom . . . the blessings of the healing art, which Christian men can rarely, if ever, bear to females of those lands. . . ." Women were, moreover, better at midwifery than men. In Boston, where male midwifery prevailed, in one out of every fourteen births the child was born dead, whereas in the Hospital of Maternity in Paris, under the superintendence of Madame Bevain, "a fraction over one in twenty-eight" was still born.[6] In spite of bigoted resistance, such women as Dr. Harriot K. Hunt,[7] Dr. Emily Blackwell and Dr. Elizabeth Blackwell [8] had established themselves as physicians. Women should have the right to learn any branch of knowledge.[9]

The methods used to prove the points were varied. All wrote editorials. Mrs. Hale and Mrs. Davis were logical; Mrs. Hale, practical; Mrs. Davis, often theoretical. Drs. Hasbrouck was frequently caustic. After noting that men did not wait to become fathers before practicing midwifery, she continued her editorial thus:

. . . This twaddle about female physicians is all moonshine, especially on the part of the male physicians, most of whom have entered the ranks while they were beardless boys, and might well have been

6. *Godey's Lady's Book*, vol. XL, no. 3, March 1852, pp. 185–189.
7. *The Una*, vol. III, no. 10, October 15, 1855, p. 148.
8. *The Sibyl*, vol. I, no. 21, May 1, 1857, p. 166.
9. *The Una*, vol. II, no. 11, November 1854, pp. 360–362.

told the unfitness of their position, when found in the practice of midwifery, or in the delicate examination and confidence of the female sick chamber. . . .[10]

On another occasion, Drs. Hasbrouck noted that brute force was not needed in the practice of medicine but "the strength that comes of the kind and gentle spirit, inspired by a generous purpose." [11] Even *Punch* supported the woman physician:

. . . If the head of a woman is not calculated for the formation of a diagnosis, she can at least shake it in a difficult case, as effectively as a man can; and having a softer and more musical voice than the masculine, she is better qualified than most men are for that large part of medical practice which consists in whispering comfort to invalids. . . .[12]

On the subject of coeducation in medicine, the women editors did not agree. Mrs. Hale believed that because of the nature of the subject, coeducation was undesirable.[13] Although Mrs. Swisshelm felt that ladies should patronize their own medical colleges,[14] she was pleased when women were admitted to the medical college at Cincinnati.[15] Mrs. Bloomer and Mrs. Davis favored coeducation in medicine.[16]

The work of the New England Female Medical College, opened in Boston in November 1848,[17] and of the Female Medical College of Pennsylvania, incorporated in 1849 and opened at Philadelphia in 1850,[18] were frequently described. Lecturers and faculty of the

10. *The Sibyl,* vol. I, no. 22, May 15, 1857, p. 172.

11. *Ibid.,* vol. IV, no. XIX, April 1, 1860, p. 726.

12. Quoted in *Home Journal,* whole no. 44, series of 1854, no. 44, October 28, 1854, p. 4.

13. *Godey's Lady's Book,* vol. LV, no. 6, December 1857, pp. 558–559.

14. *Pittsburgh Saturday Visiter,* vol. III, no. 15, January 4, 1851, p. 202.

15. *Ibid.,* vol. III, no. 51, January 4, 1851, p. 204.

16. *Ibid.,* vol. IV, no. 7, March 8, 1851, p. 26, and *The Una,* vol. II, no. 3, March 1854, pp. 233–234.

17. *The Una,* vol. I, no. 10, October 1853, p. 151; *Godey's Lady's Book,* vol. LI, no. 2, August 1855, pp. 178–179; vol. LIII, no. 6, December 1856, p. 560.

18. *The Sibyl,* vol. IV, no. XX, April 15, 1860, p. 370 and *Godey's Lady's Book,* vol. L, no. 6, June 1855, pp. 560–561; vol. LI, no. 4, October 1855, pp. 372–373.

Female Medical College of Pennsylvania were mentioned [19] and it was noted that it had a museum equal to that of the medical school of the University of Pennsylvania.[20] A group of women in Philadelphia organized the Ladies' Medical Missionary Society to raise funds to provide scholarships for the education of medical missionaries at the Female Medical College in Philadelphia. The name and address of the treasurer were given in the *Lady's Book*. Readers were invited to join the organization at one dollar a year and to contribute to the work.[21] By editorials,[22] news items,[23] and advertisements,[24] the ladies' magazines kept their readers informed of the progress of the two Female Medical Colleges.

Another vexing difficulty for the woman physician was securing the right to use hospital facilities. When women physicians were refused admission to the Pennsylvania Hospital in Philadelphia, Drs. Hasbrouck cried out against the "unfairness of expecting women to do well as doctors when every impediment was placed in her [sic] way. Why don't newspapers cry out against injustice? Are her rights of less importance than the southern slave's or oppressed Kansas? Must she endure all these indignities, yet passively submit to be jostled and spurned if she would strive to fit herself for something which would prove an untold blessing to humanity at large? Horace Greeley, where is your philanthropy, that it will thus cower and quietly witness such injustice to women? You have been calling upon her for help; now see that she be treated as an intelligent human being. . . ." [25] The opening of a hospital in New York in which women could practice was noted with gratitude.[26]

Women editors played no small part in helping women physicians

19. *Godey's Lady's Book*, vol. LIII, no. 6, December 1856, p. 560 and *The Una*, vol. I, no. 10, October 1853, p. 151.

20. *The Una*, vol. II, no. 3, March 1854, p. 233.

21. *Godey's Lady's Book*, vol. XLIV, no. 3, March 1852, pp. 185–188.

22. *The Lily*, vol. II, no. 6, June 1850, p. 45.

23. *Ibid.*, vol. V, no. 11, June 1, 1853, p. 4.

24. *Ibid.*, vol. V, no. 15, August 1, 1853, p. 4; vol. V, no. 16, August 15, 1854, p. 117.

25. *The Sibyl*, vol. I, no. 12, December 15, 1856, p. 91.

26. *Ibid.*, vol. I, no. 4, August 15, 1856, p. 31 and no. 21, May 1, 1857, p. 166, and *Godey's Lady's Book*, vol. LV, no. 3, September 1857, p. 277.

in their struggle for recognition and for a medical education. No means, even including fiction,[27] was neglected in promoting this cause. Eliakim Littell was one of the few men to show interest in the movement and "clipped" from *Eliza Cook's Journal,* an English publication, a lengthy article on "Female Doctors," which was largely devoted to a description of the Female Medical College at Philadelphia.

. . . We perceive that a Miss Elizabeth Blackwell, who received a Doctor of Medicine at Geneva College and has since pursued her medical studies at Paris, is a candidate for the professorship of surgery and other ladies offer themselves to fill other chairs. At first sight, this seems an extraordinary proceeding, and quite a startling novelty. But there are really sufficient grounds for the movement, and we hope it will succeed. For one thing it opens a new field for the employment of women, profitably and useful; and any enlargement of the field of honorable occupation for the sex tends to her own advancement, as well as that of human kind. . . .[28]

It might seem as if the woman physician were well on the road to success before the Civil War, but in reality the struggle for opportunity and recognition had just begun,—a struggle which she shared with the woman dentist. In 1858, there was a notice that an English dentist in New York planned to teach dentistry to females;[29] but, apart from this mention, the ladies' magazines seem unaware of the opportunities for women in the field of dentistry.

Nursing, another allied vocation, claimed some attention. While many women seem to have persisted in the idea that a "human heart" was the chief, if not the only, qualification for a nurse,[30] the opportunity for training at the New England Female Medical College to be a registered nurse was clearly brought out.[31] The magazines also stressed the necessity of mothers having a knowledge of physiol-

27. *Godey's Lady's Book,* vol. XLIX, no. 3, October 1854, pp. 352–355.
28. *Littell's Living Age,* vol. XXVII, no. 341, 30 November 1850, pp. 403–404.
29. *The Sibyl,* vol. II, no. 17, March 1, 1858, p. 328.
30. *Godey's Lady's Book,* vol. LX, May 1860, p. 467.
31. *Ibid.,* vol. LI, no. 4, October 1855, pp. 372–373.

ogy and anatomy.[32] In fact, no phase of medicine or medical training for women, as then known, was omitted from the pages of the ladies' magazines.

These women editors were a boon to the woman physician and championed her medical colleges. But men editors of magazines for ladies, literary journals, and educational periodicals, held aloof.

32. *Pittsburgh Saturday Visiter*, vol. II, no. 1, January 20, 1849, p. 2 and no. 3, February 3, 1849, p. 10.

CHAPTER ELEVEN

Postscript on Male Education

I N the magazines for ladies and often in their literary "Cotemporaries," information about education, exclusively for boys was a mere postscript. Three topics were discussed.

First, advice was given to the mother of the college boy. She should give her son a Bible and urge him to read it. She should write frequently to him, inquire about his health, his friends, his studies, his Church connections. She should make his visits home pleasant.[1]

Second, information about colleges was given both to the mothers in the magazines for ladies and to fathers in the general periodicals. "The Conditions and Wants of Harvard College" were discussed.[2] Comments were made on Columbia College,[3] the College of Charleston, South Carolina,[4] Yale, Dartmouth,[5] and the University of Pennsylvania.[6] It was noted that the University of Michigan formed the "necessary culminating point of popular education," [7] and that the University of Mississippi made liberal provision for the "gratuitous education of indigent men." [8]

Sometimes local pride was shown. In 1834 the *Philadelphia Album*

1. *Mothers' Magazine*, vol. XIV (no month given), 1846, pp. 334–336.
2. *North American Review*, vol. LX, no. CXXVI, January 1845, pp. 38–63 (Article II).
3. *Home Journal*, series for 1854, no. 30, whole no. 441, July 22, 1854, p. 2 (editorial).
4. *DeBow's Review and Industrial Resources, Statistics, etc.*, vol. XXII, third series, vol. II, May 1857, pp. 505–508.
5. *Philadelphia Album and Ladies' Literary Gazette*, vol. II, no. 33, January 16, 1828, p. 261.
6. *Ibid.*, vol. IV, no. 32, August 7, 1830, p. 255; vol. V, no. 7, February 12, 1831, p. 53; vol. VIII, no. 9, March 1, 1834, pp. 68–69.
7. *DeBow's Review and Industrial Resources, Statistics, etc.*, vol. XVIII, o.s., vol. I, n.s., no. 3, March 1855, pp. 425–426.
8. *Ibid.*, vol. XXVII, o.s., vol. II, n.s., no. 3, September 1859, pp. 353–358.

stated that the "University of Pennsylvania had no superior in the country." [9] Nearly twenty years later the Central High School of Philadelphia was looked upon as a "college for the people," for its departments embraced "ancient and modern languages, including the Anglo-Saxon dialect; theoretical and practical mathematics, and astronomy; natural philosophy and chemistry; anatomy, physiology, special physics, and natural history; mental, moral and political sciences; Belles-Lettres and English literature, &c. But, at the same time [it had] a department . . . devoted exclusively to penmanship, book-keeping and drawing. . . ." The B.A. and M.A. were given at semi-annual commencements.[10]

At other times loyalty was coupled with fear. In "Home Education and the South," the writer cried out against the way Southern sons were "crowding Dartmouth and Harvard, and Brown and Yale, and Amherst and Middlebury and Hamilton," where he felt they were not being guided "to light, and knowledge, and *truth*." He hoped the South would send her sons to her own institutions and no longer "unnaturally wean them." [11] The Society for the Promotion of Collegiate and Theological Education for the West reported progress in Western Reserve, Illinois, Marietta, Wittenberg and Beloit.[12] An enthusiastic writer in *The Pioneer* was sure that Santa Clara College would soon rival Harvard, Yale, Williams and Union. Santa Clara College was one of the many examples of the way in which California had "outstripped the ordinary rate of promise." [13]

Finally, changes in the plans of educating young men were noted in the reviews. These changes met with interest, if not with approval.

9. *Philadelphia Album and Ladies' Literary Gazette,* vol. VIII, no. 9, March 1, 1834, p. 69.

10. *Sartain's Union Magazine of Literature and Art,* vol. VIII, no. 4, April 1851, pp. 286–287. (John S. Hart, president of the Central High School, was one of the editors at the time.)

11. *DeBow's Review of the Southern and Western States,* vol. X, o.s., second series, vol. IV, third series, vol. II, no. 3, March 1851, pp. 362–363. The same idea is given in an article on the University of Virginia in *Southern Literary Messenger,* vol. VIII, no. 1, January 1842, pp. 50–54, and in the *Southern Quarterly Review,* vol. II, no. 4, October 1842, pp. 421 ff.

12. *Western Literary Messenger,* vol. IV, no. 1, March 1850, p. 5.

13. *The Pioneer or California Monthly,* vol. II, no. 3, September 1854, pp. 179–180.

The "bold innovation" set forth by President Wayland in his "Report to the Corporation of Brown University on Changes in the System of Collegiate Education" was fully discussed. The significant terms provided "that the various courses should be so arranged, that in so far as practicable, every student might study what he chose, and nothing but what he chose." The writer in the *North American Review* felt that the whole system of "general education" was challenged and wondered whether it would be "practicable, or if practicable, whether it would be a useful matter." [14] Adverse criticism of changes in college education was not new. Even as late as 1842 a writer in the *Southern Literary Messenger* decried the impracticable system of discipline which Jefferson had instituted at the University of Virginia. It "undertook to conduct a body of youth by appeals to their reason, their hopes, and to every generous feeling, rather than to the fear of punishment or the dread of disgrace." [15] Writers in the reviews wished to keep college education as it had been. It was exclusively "male" education.

14. *North American Review,* vol. LXXII, no. CL, January 1851, pp. 60–64.
15. *Southern Literary Messenger,* vol. VI, no. 1, January 1842, pp. 50–54 (quotation p. 52).

CHAPTER TWELVE

Conclusions

FOR this study the ideas on education have been culled from the magazines for ladies and the literary periodicals of a century ago. They have been literally gleaned from the miscellaneous matter discussed in "Editors' Tables" and "Chit-Chat," from "cards" of advertisements and book reviews, and from "fillers," placed strategically throughout the magazines. At times education was the subject of leading articles and editorials. Education was treated both with the casualness given to an old friend, and with the dignity accorded to a subject profoundly respected. It seems surprising that so many ideas on education were presented in magazines which sought primarily to entertain.

Yet it is not surprising, for education was one of the great reforms of the age. A hundred years ago, in our growing democracy, common folk had faith that they could attain that equality which they envisioned, through gaining political rights and through education. In education, they saw a great equalizing force—a force through which the individual could become the equal of anyone in the community, a force through which labor could attain a new dignity, a force through which reforms could be accomplished. To woman denied political rights, education offered the one hope and the one means.

Editors, solely dependent upon a paid circulation for the financial support of their periodicals, were not unmindful of this interest. How far they were so stimulated by it, or how far they directed their readers' attention to educational matters, there is no way of knowing. But at least one editor of a ladies' magazine was recognized by her contemporaries for her educational leadership. In 1860 the Baltimore Female College gave a medal to "Mrs. Sarah Josepha Hale,

the editress of Godey's Lady's Book for her distinguished service
in the cause of education." [1]

Nor was this medal undeserved, for Mrs. Hale lost no opportunity
to show the need and desirability of educating women, and to champion public schools, elementary and high schools, state supported
colleges and federally supported normal schools. Mrs. Hale was not
alone in her activity; but perhaps because *Godey's* was looked upon
as "the book of the nation" and because her work as editor lasted
for forty-three years, her leadership was recognized.

Magazines generally supported free elementary education. Even
in the Southern magazines which made clear that free education
should not be given to slaves, the ideal of public elementary education
was endorsed. Many editors supported free high schools, but several
Southern writers did not join their Northern and Western brethren.
Only a few editors of popular periodicals, notably Mrs. Hale,
Mrs. Swisshelm and Mrs. Davis, advocated free normal schools.
Editors of such different periodicals as *The Lily, The Lady's Book,*
and the *Southern Literary Messenger* wanted a state college.

The endorsement of educational opportunities for women was a
different matter. Here there was a cleavage along sex lines. The
men editors frequently gave pen service to the cause of woman's
education; but the enthusiasm and persistence characteristic of the
women editors was lacking. There was a whole-heartedness about
the women's support of education for girls, whether it took the form
of the erudite expositions of *The Una,* the simple logic of *The Lily,*
the barbed thrusts of the *Pittsburgh Saturday Visiter* and *The Sibyl,*
or the free advertising of schools for girls and the innumerable articles
on their education in *The Lady's Book.* Mrs. Davis, Mrs. Bloomer,
Mrs. Swisshelm, Drs. Hasbrouck and Mrs. Hale may not have agreed
on the kind of education girls should receive, but they did all in their
power to see that opportunities in education were provided. In advo-
cating the education of women doctors these women editors stood
four square behind woman physicians. No man editor gave even pen
service to this cause.

1. *Godey's Lady's Book,* vol. LX, no. 6, June 1860, p. 468.

All the ladies' magazines, especially those edited by the clergy, gave specific suggestions for the training of children. The magazines for ladies were themselves the educators. Most of the suggestions dealt with the formation of a fine character. While the general periodicals discussed the aims of education in the same lofty terms as the magazines for ladies, they gave no advice to mothers on the training of their children.

There were two other groups of magazines which alone endorsed certain phases of education. The editors of the *Southern Literary Messenger,* the *Southern Quarterly Review* and *DeBow's Review* urged the South to develop her own schools and colleges and to secure Southern writers for textbooks in order that Southern institutions might be preserved. The editors of publications in German pointed out the need for German youth to use German in schools if German culture was to continue in America.

Thus popular periodicals took definite positions on educational developments. With respect to the philosophy of education, however, there was often as great a diversity of opinion within a magazine as between magazines.

As important as estimating the possible educational leadership of these magazines is determining the extent to which they presented a well-rounded picture of educational developments. There are two ways of doing this: first, by comparing the ideas presented in the lay periodicals with those in the contemporary educational journals; second, by comparing them with ideas deemed important by twentieth century writers of the history of education.

To compare point by point the phases of education discussed in the general and professional periodicals would constitute a restatement of material. A simpler way is to note educational topics which were not included in both groups of magazines. First may be noted those included in the popular periodicals and excluded from the educational journals. A question, debated at length in the magazines for gentlemen as well as those for ladies, was that moot one of whether woman had a brain like that of man. This question crept into the educational periodicals, not as a subject of debate or con-

sideration, but as a springboard for attacking the superficial education provided for girls.[2]

Second, those phases of education which were frequently discussed
in educational periodicals and were hardly touched upon in popular
magazines. Plans for school buildings were an important feature
of the educational magazines in the fifties.[3] The few reviews that
presented an occasional picture were more interested in cost than
in architecture; [4] and the magazines for ladies, especially *Godey's,*
were too intent upon giving plans for *the one home* to consider that
for a school.[5] Methods of teaching and the arrangement of a class
were important to the educator-editors. Except in the management
of children, method was seldom mentioned by the editors of the
popular periodicals. Plans for school buildings and methods of
teaching may have been too technical to interest the general
reader.

Occasionally the same matter was presented in lay and professional periodicals but in a different way and with a different purpose.
Nowhere is this better illustrated than in the accounts of Laura
Bridgman, the blind, deaf-mute. To editors of ladies' magazines, she
was a wonderful person to be described to their readers. To educators, Laura was wonderful; but her prowess was used as a means
to inspire teachers of normal children. A similar distinction might be
noted in the treatment of the great European leaders of education,—
Rousseau, Pestalozzi, Fellenberg and Froebel. To educators, descriptions of their work were vital in order to interpret philosophy and
method to the teacher-readers.[6] A few laymen saw these educational
implications; but for the most part, descriptions of Howfyl or a
Froebel kindergarten and of such American counterparts as the

2. *Common School Journal,* vol. IX, no. 19, October 1, 1847, p. 298 (article,
"Uneducated Women," pp. 297–298).

3. For example, "Description of Public High School in Philadelphia" by
John S. Hart in *American Journal of Education,* vol. I, no. 1, August 1855,
pp. 93–102.

4. *Frank Leslie's Illustrated Newspaper,* vol. II, no. 27, June 14, 1856,
p. 13; vol. I, no. 18, April 13, 1856, p. 285.

5. *Godey's Lady's Book,* vol. XLVI, no. 2, February 1853, p. 102; no. 4,
April 1853, p. 292; no. 5, May 1853, p. 388, etc.

6. *Common School Journal,* vol. IV, no. 10, May 16, 1842, pp. 145 ff.

schools at Perth Amboy, New Jersey, and Sharon, Pennsylvania, were pictorial, rather than philosophic.

At times, phases of education attained the dignity of consideration in the popular periodicals, as in the discussion of what constituted an education, an appreciation of the work of the teacher, or the condemnation of the radical elective system at Brown.

Most of the editors reprinted, summarized, and commented upon reports of superintendents, especially those of Horace Mann and Henry Barnard, and speeches and articles by such distinguished educators as F. A. P. Barnard and Catharine Beecher. Here were treated in a lucid manner such topics as the common school, education of women and the function of the state in providing higher as well as elementary education. Thus those reforms which needed the support of the common man and the "influence" of the common woman were brought to their attention. With the exception of what might be called the technical aspects of education, the ladies' magazines and the literary periodicals gave to their readers a remarkably well-rounded picture of educational developments of the time. They assisted the editors of the professional journals in their educational campaigns. Often they did it so casually that their readers were probably unaware of their intent.

When the ideas on education presented to the ladies and gentlemen of a century ago are compared with those of the twentieth-century histories of education, they seem both significant and comprehensive. With the exception of the discussion of the change in method, all phases of educational development were touched upon in the popular periodicals. It is apparent that the magazines for ladies and their contemporaries presented a well-rounded picture of education. They made a real if humble contribution to the development of education in America.

It is interesting, also, to note the manner of discussion of educational problems between 1830 and 1860. Where ideas are considered, there is very little difference between the opinions of 1830 and of 1860. Where the concrete manifestation of these ideas is pictured, there is a decided change. In 1830 Mrs. Hale wrote about the desirability of educating girls. In the 1840's and 1850's she campaigned for high schools for girls. In the 1850's and in the 1860's, federally supported normal schools and colleges for women were the subject of her dissertations. What Mrs. Hale's *Ladies' Magazine* and the *Lady's Book* show in bold relief, was true of most magazines for ladies.

As a specific goal was gained, they set a new goal, while theoretical discussions continued in much the same terms. Educational advance, as seen in magazines for ladies, was made in specific steps and not by change in ideas. Nor was this method of progress confined to the ladies. General periodicals show the same trend, but because they were not so devoted to any phase of education as were the ladies' magazines to the education of girls, the trend is not so pronounced.

The modern reader, however, is interested in the ideas themselves and in the reasoning of these writers of another age. He sees twentieth-century counterparts in many of these ideas on education, especially in the definition of education. Robert Maynard Hutchins and the Neo-Thomists, as well as many Catholic educators with their Aristotelian and scholastic philosophy probably have more in common with these mid-nineteenth century predecessors than with many of their twentieth-century contemporaries.[7] Those who deem themselves in the vanguard of educational thought and demand the education of the "whole child" echo the magazines for ladies. The idea of the farm school is at least a hundred years old. Even Hitler and the many twentieth-century propagandists, who have seen in education a means of promoting and preserving a state of their dreams, have their counterpart both in the Southern writers who saw clearly the necessity of indoctrinating Southern youth in an appreciation of the desirability of slavery and in the plea of the editors of German magazines for the perpetuation of German culture.

The twentieth-century reader is interested also in the reasoning of the writers of a century ago. When the reader is feminine, she either smiles or becomes angry at the "twaddle" about woman's "sphere" and rejoices that it is a thing of the past. But is it? The

7. Merle Curti, *The Growth of American Thought* (Harper and Brothers Publishers, New York, 1943, xx, 848 pp.), pp. 733–734.

constant discussion in newspapers, magazines and over the radio
of whether a married woman should work is an aspect of the "sphere."
There is an important difference, however. In the twentieth century,
the woman herself is expected to have an opinion. Those who are
consulted or interviewed are often women. Men, however, take an
important part in the discussion. A discriminating reader can see in
the writings of such an authority on women and the family as the
sociologist, Ernest Rutherford Groves of the University of North
Carolina, a recognition of the intellectual, economic, political, and
legal equality of women, but at the same time a belief that women are
emotionally dependent upon men.[8] Is this not a twentieth-century
slant to the nineteenth-century "sphere"?

The relation between the races is becoming as much discussed as
the relation between the sexes. In the United Stats are there not
some who think in terms of "sphere" for the Negroes? If in the following quotation "woman" is substituted for "Negro" and "man"
for "white man," it seems as if it had been taken from a magazine
of the 1830's rather than from one in the 1930's.

. . . As every child needs a loving parent, so every Negro under
our civilization needs a white man as his protective genius, his
guardian angel—his master, not in the offensive imperious sense, but
in the patriarchal and kindly one. In the South (and occasionally in
the North) the Negro nearly always has such a friend. But in the
South this relationship is the custom, while in the North it is rare,
accidental, and not very effective.

The true Negro has a great gift for estimating character, for discerning human values. He has always known that the white man was
created superior, or at least different; and this fact he accepts as a
law of nature, as he does the rising of the sun, the mighty rhythm
of the seasons, the antiphonal chanting of the tides. A Negro is seldom
impressed by what a white man does, for the simple reason that he
expects high achievements from one in a lofty station. God's works
do not surprise us; they merely fulfill our idea of His limitless power.
In much the same way the Negro regards the lordly entrances and

8. This is especially true in Ernest Rutherford Groves, *The American
Woman, the Feminine Side of a Masculine Civilization* (New York, Green-
berg, 1937, 438 pp.).

performances and exits of the white man. On the other hand, when the white man fails, even in a too heroic undertaking, the Negro stands mutely amazed. He appears to find that nature has failed to function. . . .[9]

At times writers in the two centuries have reached the same conclusion. Two such different people as Mrs. Sarah Josepha Hale, the editress of *Godey's Lady's Book* and Dr. Paul R. Mort of Teachers College, Columbia University, the Inglis lecturer for 1943, advocated that women teachers should receive lower wages than men teachers. Mrs. Hale felt that women were better teachers for young children than men. She never accepted the idea that woman's intelligence was inferior to that of man; it was simply "different." Their moral influence, and this to Mrs. Hale was most important, was far superior. Woman, she thought, could afford to work for lower wages than man. She was realistic enough to recognize that it was impossible to find young men who would become teachers for such meager compensation instead of answering the call of the West.[10] Dr. Mort is equally realistic. He believes that because of the meager salaries paid to teachers, the finest men do not enter the teaching profession. He thinks it desirable that boys be taught by men. To attract fine men, it is necessary to pay higher salaries. Since most schools can not afford to raise the salaries of all teachers, the only alternative is to raise those of men. Thus better men will be secured for the teaching profession.[11] Both Mrs. Hale and Dr. Mort are interested primarily in the welfare of the children; both are mindful of economics. The opinion of each has been challenged. Mrs. Davis took issue with Mrs. Hale in *The Una*.[12] That there are many today who believe in equal pay for equal work need hardly be mentioned.

When the conclusions and the logic supporting them are compared

9. Archibald Rutledge, "The Negro in the North" in *The South Atlantic Quarterly,* vol. XXXI, no. 1, January 1932, pp. 61–62 (entire article pp. 61–69).

10. *Godey's Lady's Book,* vol. XLV, no. 2, August 1852, p. 193.

11. Paul R. Mort, *The Inglis Lecture, 1943, Secondary Education as Public Policy* (Cambridge, Massachusetts, Harvard University Press, 1943, 85 pp.), especially pp. 77–79.

12. *The Una,* vol. II, no. 2, February 1854, pp. 218–219.

across the century, it seems as if we were intellectually marking time. But this is not the case. Common schools, public high schools, state systems of education crowned by state universities, education of women, the liberalization of the curriculum,—these have been accomplished. The fact that old techniques and old arguments are used for new problems need not cause discouragement. These techniques did not hinder progress in the past; they may have helped it. It is natural so long as the medium remains the same, that is the printed page of the magazine. As the ladies' magazines of a century ago reached a newly discovered audience and unleashed an unexpected force of public opinion, it is quite possible that radio's discovery of the listening hours of the woman on the farm and of the house-wife and mother, may again bring the problems of education into the home.

Bibliographical Essay

MAGAZINES

The primary sources for this study have been the magazines themselves. They are listed according to alphabet. Their titles, dates, places of issue, their editors and their character during the period 1830–1860, have been given. Only those holdings of libraries which are not fully indicated in the *Union List of Serials in Libraries of the United States and Canada,* Second Edition, Edited by Winifred Gregory (New York, The H. H. Wilson Company, 1943) are noted.

Advocate of Moral Reform, the bi-monthly organ of the American Female Guardian Society and Home for Friendless, New York (called the New York Female Moral Reform Society 1835–1837 and Female Moral Reform Society 1841–1845). While the title varies slightly, it was called *Advocate of Moral Reform* from 1832 until 1887, when the title was changed to *Advocate and Family Guardian.* It is still published in New York. At first it was edited by members of the society, assisted by clergymen. Miss Sarah Towne Smith, who became Mrs. Martyn in 1841, was editor from 1836 until 1845. She was followed by Helen E. Brown, Mrs. S. R. I. Bennett and others.

Abendschule, Ein Deutsches Familienblatt, Die, published in Buffalo from 1854 to 1856 and in St. Louis by L. Lange from 1856 to 1940.

American Annals of Education see *American Journal of Education.*

American Journal of Education is the first important American magazine in the field of education. It was called: *American Journal of Education,* January 1826—May, 1830; *American Journal of Education and Monthly Lyceum,* June and July 1830; *American Journal and Annals of Education and Instruction,* August–December, 1830; *American Annals of Education* and *Instruction and Journal of Literary Instructions, being a continuation of the American Journal of Education,* 1831; *American Annals of Education,* 1832–1839. For the most part it was a monthly and was always published in Boston. The editors included: William Russell, 1826–1828; James G. Carter, 1829–1831; William C. Woodbridge, 1831–1836; William A. Alcott and William C. Woodbridge, 1837; William A. Alcott, 1838; and M. F. Hubbard, 1839.

American Journal of Education was edited by Henry Barnard from August 1855 until 1882. Absalom Peters was co-editor of the first two numbers of the first volume. Although usually a quarterly, it was published irregularly in New York and Hartford, Conn. Largely because of its editor, it is considered the best of the educational magazines. It was known as: *The American Journal of Education and College Review,* August 1855–January 1856; *The American Journal of Education,* March 1856–1882.

American Ladies' Magazine see Ladies' Magazine.

American Whig Review, a Whig Journal of Politics, Literature, Art and Science, a monthly published in New York from January 1845 to December 1852. Sub-title varies.

Amerikanisch-Deutsche Hausfreund und Baltimore Calendar auf das Jahr Schrift, Der, published in German at Baltimore by John T. Hansche, between 1835 and 1844 was like an almanac, with items of history, especially about the Middle Ages, and information about Courts of Quarter Session and Common Pleas in Maryland, Virginia, and Pennsylvania.

Arthur's Home Magazine, a monthly published in Philadelphia at two dollars a year from October 1852 until December 1898. The titles include: *The Home Magazine,* with running head, *Arthur's Home Magazine,* 1852–1854; *Arthur's Home Magazine,* 1854–1856, 1861–1871, 1880–1891; *The Lady's Home Magazine,* with running head, *Arthur's Home Magazine,* 1857–1860. T. S. Arthur was editor from 1852 to 1885, and was assisted by Virginia F. Townsend, 1855 to 1872.

Atlantic Monthly, a literary monthly, published in Boston from November 1857 to the present. The title from 1857 to September 1865 was *The Atlantic Monthly; a Magazine of Litera-*

ture, Art and Politics. Then it became *The Atlantic Monthly; A Magazine of Literature, Science, Art and Politics.* James Russell Lowell was editor from 1857 to June 1861.

Atlantis, Eine Monatschrift Für Wissenschaft, Politik und Poesie, edited and published by Christian Esselen of Buffalo, New York, 1856–1858.

Ballou's Pictorial Drawing-Room Companion see *Gleason's Pictorial Drawing-Room Companion.*

Belletristiches Journal, Eine Wochenschrift für Literatur, Kunst, Wissenschaft, Politik und Tagesgeschichte, published in New York from 1852 to 1909.

Biene, Ein Volks-Blatt, Die, edited by Reverend A. L. Heubner, a Moravian clergyman and published in Bethlehem from 1846 to 1848. A file is at the Moravian Archives, Bethlehem, Pennsylvania.

Blätter für Freies Religiöses Leben, edited by Friedrich Schünemann-Pott in 1859. Published as a volume in 1860 in Philadelphia. This may be found at the Carl Schurz Foundation, Philadelphia.

Brüder Blatt, Das, a monthly edited by Moravian clergy,—the Reverend Levin T. Reichel of Lititz, Pennsylvania (1854) and of Salem, North Carolina (1855 and 1856) and others; published in Lancaster, Pennsylvania from 1854 to 1857. File at the Moravian Archives at Bethlehem, Pennsylvania.

Chicago Magazine, published twice a month in Chicago from March 1857 to June 15, 1857.

Cincinnati Mirror and Ladies' Parterre, edited by William D. Gallagher in Cincinnati from October 1, 1831 to September 17, 1836.

Columbian Lady's and Gentleman's Magazine, Embracing Literature in Every Department: Embellished with the Finest Steel and Mezzotint Engravings, Music and Colored Fashions was published monthly in New York City from January 1844 to February 1849. The editors included: John Inman, 1844; John Inman and Robert A. West, 1845–April 1848; Stephen M. Chester, May–December, 1848; Darius Mead, 1849.

Common School Assistant, a monthly, published in Albany from 1836 to 1840. It was edited by J. Orville Taylor and gave educational news of New York state.

Common School Journal, a semi-monthly, published in Boston from 1836 to 1852. Horace Mann was editor from 1836 to 1849; William B. Fowle, from 1849 to 1852.

Common School Journal of the State of Pennsylvania, published under the supervision of the Superintendent of Common Schools of the Commonwealth on the fifteenth of each month during 1844 at Philadelphia and Harrisburg. It was edited by John S. Hart, Principal of the Central High School, Philadelphia.

Connecticut Common School Journal, published under the direction of the Board of Commissioners of Common Schools at Hartford, from 1838 to 1853 when Henry Barnard was editor. From 1854 on, a committee of the Connecticut State Teachers' Association assisted in the editing. Barnard was editor-in-chief in 1855. From 1856 to 1859 inclusive, the members of the committee took turns editing different issues. From 1854 to 1866 it was published by the State Teachers' Association of Connecticut and was known from 1854 to 1858 as *The Connecticut Common School Journal and Annals of Education.* It was published irregularly.

DeBow's Review, a monthly published from January 1846 to June 1880. From 1846 to 1867 James D. B. DeBow was editor and publisher. The titles include: *The Commercial Review of the South and West,* 1846; *DeBow's Commercial Review of the South and West,* 1847–1850; *DeBow's Review of the Southern and Western States,* 1850–1852; *DeBow's Review and Industrial Resources, Statistics, etc.,* 1853–1864. It was published at New Orleans from 1846 to 1852 and from 1859 to 1861 and at Washington from 1853 to 1858, when DeBow was superintendent of the census.

Deutsch-Amerikanische Didaskalia, Vierteljahrschrift, Für Geist, Gemüth und Publicität der Deutschen in den Vereinigten Staaten. Published in Baltimore by Friedrich Raine in 1848.

Dial, The: A Magazine for Literature, Philosophy, Religion, a quarterly, published in Boston from July 1840 to April 1844. Margaret Fuller was editor from July 1840 to April 1842; Ralph Waldo Emerson from July 1842 to April 1844. It was the organ of the transcendentalist group.

District School Journal for the State of New York, a monthly publication subsidized by the state from 1840 to 1852. The title was changed to *District School Journal of the State of New York* in 1847.

Family Magazine; Weekly Abstract of Knowledge, published irregularly in New York from April 20, 1833 to May 1841.

France Littéraire, La, published monthly in New York from 1834 to 1836 inclusive. It was listed as *France Littéraire.*

Frank Leslie's Illustrated Newspaper, a weekly published in New York from 1855 to 1891; continued under other titles until 1922.

Frank Leslie's Illustrated Newspaper, a weekly published in New from August 15, 1857 to 1889.

Frank Leslie's New Family Magazine, a monthly, published in New York from September 1857 to December 1882. It was edited by Frank Leslie from 1857 to 1863.

Free Enquirer, The, a weekly published in New York from March 4, 1829 to June 28, 1835. It was the successor to *The New-Harmony Gazette* and was edited from 1829 to October 1832 by Frances Wright and Robert Dale Owen; Owen's brother-in-law, H. D. Robinson was editor the last two and a half years.

Friend of Virtue, the bimonthly organ of the Female Moral Reform Society of Boston from 1838 to 1867. From 1867 to 1892, it was known as *Home Guardian.* Miss Rebecca Eaton, the corresponding secretary, became editor in 1838 and continued for many years.

Frontier Monthly, published at Hastings, Minnesota, April, May and June 1859.

Gleason's Pictorial Drawing Room Companion (1851–1854) became *Ballou's Pictorial Drawing Room Companion* (1855–1859). Maturin M. Ballou was editor; Frederick Gleason, publisher 1851–1854; Ballou, 1854–1859. Published weekly in Boston.

Godey's Lady's Book, a monthly, published in Philadelphia from 1830 to 1898. The titles include: *The Lady's Book,* 1830–1839; *Godey's Lady's Book and Ladies' American Magazine,* 1840–1843; *Godey's Magazine and Lady's Book,* 1844–1848; *Godey's Lady's Book,* 1848–1854, 1883–1892; *Godey's Lady's Book and Magazine,* 1854–1883. From 1830 to 1837 Louis A. Godey was editor; from 1837 to 1877, Louis A. Godey and Mrs. Sarah

Josepha Hale; between 1839 and 1845, Mrs. Lydia H. Sigourney and Morton McMichael assisted at times.

Graham's Magazine, a monthly published in Philadelphia from January 1826 to December 1858. The titles include: *The Casket: Flowers of Literature, Wit and Sentiment,* 1826–1838; *The Casket and Philadelphia Monthly Magazine, Embracing Every Department of Literature; Embellished with Engravings, the Quarterly Fashions, and Music, Arranged for the Piano-Forte, Harp and Guitar,* 1839–1840; *Graham's Lady's and Gentleman's Magazine (The Casket and Gentleman's United). Embracing Every Department of Literature: Embellished with Engravings, Fashions and Music, Arranged for the Piano-Forte, Harp and Guitar,* 1841–1842; July 1843–June 1844; *Graham's American Monthly Magazine of Literature and Art,* July 1848–June 1856; *Graham's Illustrated Magazine of Literature, Romance, Art and Fashion,* July 1856–1858. The editors include: Samuel C. Atkinson, 1826–1839; George R. Graham, 1839–1853. The following editors assisted Graham: Charles J. Peterson and Edgar Allan Poe, 1839–1842 (Poe resigned in May); Mrs. Emma C. Embury and Mrs. Ann S. Stephens, 1842; Rufus W. Griswold, May 1842–October 1843; Robert T. Conrad, J. R. Chandler, and J. Bayard Taylor, during the year 1848. Charles Godfrey Leland edited it from 1853 to 1858.

Harper's Monthly Magazine, a monthly magazine published by Harper and Brothers, New York from June 1850 until the present. From 1850 to 1900, it was called *Harper's New Monthly Magazine;* in 1900, the "New" was dropped and since 1925, it has been known simply as *Harper's Magazine.* Henry J. Raymond was editor from 1850 to 1856; Alfred H. Guernsey from 1856 to 1869.

Home Journal, The, a weekly, published in New York from 1846 to the present. The titles include: *The National Press: A Home Journal,* February 14 to November 14, 1846; *The Home Journal,* November 21, 1846 to March 23, 1901; *Town and Country,* 1901 to the present. George Pope Morris and Nathaniel Parker Willis were editors from 1846 to 1864.

Hutchings' Illustrated California Magazine, a monthly published by James M. Hutchings in San Francisco from July 1856 to 1861.

Journal of the Rhode Island Institute of Instruction, edited by Henry Barnard, Commissioner of Public Schools of Rhode Island and published irregularly from 1845 to 1848 in Providence.

Knickerbocker, The, a monthly published in New York from January 1833 to October 1865. Between 1833 and 1862 it was entitled *The Knickerbocker; or, New-York Monthly Magazine.* In the first volume, it was spelled "Knickerbacker." The editors included: Charles Fenno Hoffman, January–March 1833; Samuel Daly Langtree, April 1833–April 1834; and Timothy Flint, co-editor October 1833–February 1834 (he edited March 1834 alone); Lewis Gaylord Clark, May 1834–1860. (Willis Gaylord Clark, associate editor, 1834–1841.)

Ladies' Companion, The, a monthly, published in New York from May 1834 to October 1844 by William W. Snowden. Snowden was editor from 1834 to 1843, when he secured the services of Mrs. Lydia H. Sigourney, Mrs. Emma C. Embury and others. The titles included: *The Ladies' Companion; A Monthly Magazine Embracing Every Department of Literature, Embellished with Original Engravings and Music Arranged for the Piano Forte, Harp and Guitar,* 1834–1843; *The Ladies' Companion, and Literary Expositor: A Monthly Magazine Embracing* (as above) 1843–1844.

Ladies' Garland, published irregularly from April 15, 1837 to June 1849 at Philadelphia. The titles vary greatly. Some of the forms are: *Ladies' Garland and Family Wreath, Embracing Tales, Sketches, Incidents, History, Poetry, Music;* in many issues, *Ladies' Garland: A Wreath of Many Flowers, Devoted to Literature, Amusement and Instruction* (1837 and 1838); *The Ladies' Garland and Dollar Magazine, a Monthly Journal,* 1847–1849. Samuel D. Patterson was editor and publisher from 1847 to 1849.

Ladies' Gift and Souvenir of Friendship, The, Illustrated with Engravings, an annual, published in Boston by David P. King, 1850 and 1851, 324 pp. The only difference between the two volumes is the date.

Ladies' Magazine, a monthly, published in Boston and edited by Mrs. Sarah Josepha Hale from 1828 to 1836. The titles include: *The Ladies' Magazine,* 1828–1829, 1833; *The Ladies' Magazine and Literary Gazette,* 1830–1832; *American Ladies' Magazine,* 1834–1836.

Ladies' Miscellany, published irregularly for one dollar a year at Salem, Massachusetts. Volume I, number 1 was dated Friday, November 7, 1828. It seems to have continued until June 9, 1833.

Ladies' Parlor Companion, The: A Collection of Scattered Fragments and Literary Gems, an annual, edited by E. Hutchinson and published in New York in 1852 (408 pp.).

Ladies' Pearl, a monthly, edited by the Reverend Daniel Wise and published in Lowell, Massachusetts from 1841 to 1843, inclusive. The full title was *The Ladies' Pearl: A Monthly Magazine, Embellished with Engravings, and Original Music.* Variety was given in the spelling of "Ladies' " (Lady's).

Ladies' Repository, The, a monthly published by agents of the Methodist Book Concern at Cincinnati, from January 1841 to December 1876, and edited by Methodist clergymen. From 1841 to 1848 it was known as *The Ladies' Repository and Gatherings of the West;* from 1849 to 1876, *The Ladies' Repository,* with the subtitle, *A Monthly Periodical Devoted to Literature and Religion.*

Lady's Amaranth, a Journal of Tales, Essays, Receipts, Historical and Biographical Sketches, Poetry and Literature in General was published twice a month by Joseph Torr between 1838 and 1842 in Philadelphia. Volumes III, IV, and V have no dates.

Lady's Western Magazine and Garland of the Valley, a monthly published in 1848 and 1849 at Chicago and Milwaukee. Copies are in the University of Chicago Library.

Lily, The, A Ladies' Journal, Devoted to Temperance and Literature, a monthly from 1849 to 1852; a semi-monthly from 1853 to 1856. It was edited and published by Mrs. Amelia Bloomer from 1849 to 1854, inclusive, at Seneca Falls, New York (1849–1853) and Mt. Vernon, Ohio (1854) and by Mrs. Mary B. Birdsall at Richmond, Indiana in 1855 and 1856.

It is impossible to get a complete file of *The Lily* at any library. Volumes I to IV (1849–1852) may be read at the Library of the State of New York at Albany; volumes VI to VIII (1853–1856) at the Boston Public Library. The copy of volume V (1853) in

the possession of the Library of the State of New York has
been so badly damaged by fire that it is at present not usable.
Numbers 1, 5, 6 and 14 of volume V may be read at the New
York Public Library; numbers 3 and 4, 7 to 13 inclusive, 15
to 17 inclusive, 19 to 23 inclusive are owned by Cornell University Library. Thus, only the following numbers are lacking:
volume V, no. 2, January 15, 1853, no. 18, September 15, 1853
and no. 24, December 15, 1853.

Littell's Living Age, a weekly published in Boston, May 11, 1844–
1927; a monthly 1927 to date. From 1844 to 1870, it was edited
by Eliakim Littell. Since 1897, it has been known as *The Living
Age.*

Magnolia, The; or, Southern Apalachian, a monthly from January
1840 to June 1843. In 1840, it was known as *The Southern
Ladies' Book; a Magazine of Literature, Science and Arts* and
was published at Macon, Georgia under the editorship of George
F. Pierce and Philip C. Pendleton. In 1841–1842, it was known
as *The Magnolia; or, Southern Monthly;* was published in
Savannah, Georgia and edited by Philip C. Pendleton. In July
1842, the name was changed to *The Magnolia; or, Southern
Apalachian,* the publication office was removed to Charleston and
William Gilmore Simms became editor.

Magnolia, The; a gift book or annual, edited by Henry W. Herbert
and published in New York in 1841, 1842, 1843, and 1844 in the
same form.

Massachusetts Teacher, a monthly edited from 1848 to 1874 by a
state teachers' association.

*Miss Leslie's Magazine: Home Book of Fashion, Literature and Do-
mestic Economy,* a monthly published in Philadelphia during
1843, edited by Eliza Leslie.

Moore's Western Lady's Book, a monthly published by A. Moore
and Mrs. A. G. Moore in Cincinnati from 1850.

Moravian Church Miscellany, The, published at Bethlehem from
1850 through 1856.

Mother's Magazine, The, a monthly published in New York from
1833 to 1888. Mrs. A. G. Whittelsey was editor from 1833 to
1850; the Reverend D. Mead was co-editor 1844–1850.

Mrs. Stephens' Illustrated New Monthly, published in New York by Edward H. Stephens from 1856 to 1858.

National Anti-Slavery Standard, a weekly published in New York by the Anti-Slavery Society. During the 1840's Lydia Maria Child and her husband, David Child, were editors.

National Magazine or Ladies' Emporium, The, a monthly published in Baltimore from November 1830 through 1831. It was edited by Mrs. Mary Chase Burney.

New York Saturday Press, a weekly newspaper, published in New York from January 7, 1858 to 1866.

North American Review, The, published in Boston from May 1815 to 1877 and in New York from 1878 to 1940. It was a quarterly from December 1818 to October 1876 and was known as *The North-American Review and Miscellaneous Journal* until 1821 and since then as *The North American Review.*

Oak Leaf, The, a monthly literary magazine published by the Gnothantii Society of Knox College, Galesburg, Illinois in 1856 and 1857.

Pennsylvania Journal of Prison Discipline and Philanthropy, The, a monthly published from 1845 to 1849 inclusive under the direction of the Philadelphia Society for the Alleviation of the Miseries of Public Prisons, Instituted in 1787.

Pennsylvania School Journal, a monthly published from 1852 to the present, first at Lancaster and then at Harrisburg, frequently under the editorship of the state superintendent of schools.

Peterson's Magazine, a monthly published from January 1842 to April 1898. Until 1895, it was published at Philadelphia, when it was moved to New York. From 1842 to 1887, Charles J. Peterson was editor and publisher; Mrs. Ann S. Stephens was co-editor from 1842 to 1853. The titles included: *Ladies' National Magazine,* 1842–1848; *The Lady's World of Literature and Fashion,* 1843 (title varied); *Peterson's Magazine,* 1848; 1851–1853; 1855–1892; *Peterson's Ladies' National Magazine,* 1848–1854 (title varied).

Philadelphia Album and Ladies' Literary Gazette, a weekly published in Philadelphia from June 7, 1826 through December 1834. In 1826 it was known as *The Album.* Until June 1828, it was edited by Thomas C. Clarke; in January 1830 Robert Morris became editor. N. P. Willis was an editor of most of volume III (June 4, 1828–May 27, 1829). Volume IV began Saturday, January 2, 1830. At times the publication of this journal was very irregular.

Pioneer or California Monthly, The, a monthly literary periodical published at San Francisco in 1854 and 1855.

Pittsburgh Saturday Visiter, a weekly published in Pittsburgh from 1848 to January 17, 1852. Jane G. Swisshelm was the editor; Robert M. Riddle was co-editor of volume II (1849). There is no complete file. The Carnegie Library of Pittsburgh has the most nearly complete one; the American Antiquarian Society at Worcester has six issues not in the possession of the Carnegie Library. They are: June 22 and 29, 1850; July 20, 1850; December 6, 1851; January 17, 1852. The following issues have not been located: all of volume I (1848) except number 11, February 28, 1848; volume II, number 20, June 2, 1849; number 40, October 20, 1849; number 44, November 17, 1849; number 51, January 5, 1850; number 52, January 12, 1850; volume III, numbers 4 to 7 inclusive, February 9, 1850 to March 7, 1850; number 10, March 23, 1850; numbers 12 to 14 inclusive, April 6, 1850 to April 20, 1850; number 16, May 4, 1850; number 20, June 8, 1850; volume IV, number XIV, April 26, 1851; number XXI, June 14, 1851; number XXVIII, August 2, 1851 to number XXXI, August 23, 1851; number XXXIII, September 6, 1851; number XXXVI, September 27, 1851; number XLV, November 29, 1851.

Revue Française, La, published in New York from 1833 to 1836. Hoskins and Snowden, publishers from November 1833 to July 1836, when Alexander Debonnet became publisher.

Sargent's New Monthly Magazine of Literature, Fashion and the Fine Arts, a monthly published in New York during the first six months of 1843 by Epes Sargent.

Sartain's Union Magazine of Literature and Art, a monthly published in New York as the *Union Magazine of Literature and Art* from July 1847 to December 1848, and in Philadelphia from January 1849 to August 1852. Mrs. Caroline M. Kirkland was editor from July 1847 to June 1851; John S. Hart was co-editor from January 1849 to June 1851; Reynell Coats was editor

July–November 1851; John Sartain was editor and publisher December 1851–August 1852.

Sibyl, The, a semi-monthly July 1856–June 1861, a monthly July 1861–June 1864, published in Middletown, New York by John W. Hasbrouck. It was edited by Drs. Lydia Sayer, who in August, 1856, married her printer. The full title was *The Sibyl: A Review of the Tastes, Errors and Fashions of Society.*

Southern Lady's Companion, a monthly published in Nashville, Tennessee, from 1847 to 1854 at the office of the *Nashville and Louisville Christian Advocate.* It was edited by Methodist clergymen, most of the time by the Reverend M. M. Henkle.

Southern Literary Journal, The, a monthly review published in Charleston, South Carolina from September 1835 to December 1838. Daniel K. Whitaker, a New Englander, was editor until 1837.

Southern Literary Messenger, The, a monthly published in Richmond from August 1834 to June 1864. Its best known editor was Edgar Allan Poe from December 1835 to January 1837.

Southern Quarterly Review, The, a quarterly published from January 1842 to February 1857. During 1842 it was published at New Orleans; from 1843 to 1855 at Charleston, South Carolina; and thereafter at Columbia, South Carolina. The editors included: Daniel K. Whitaker, 1842–1847; J. Milton Clapp, 1847–1849; William Gilmore Simms, 1849–1855; James H. Thornwell, 1856–1857.

Southern Parlour Magazine, a monthly published from 1852 to 1856 at Mobile and Memphis under the editorship of W. G. C. Clark.

Southern Review, a quarterly published in Charleston, South Carolina from 1828 to 1832.

Southern Rose, The, published every two weeks at Charleston, South Carolina from 1832–1839. It was known as *The Southern Rosebud* the first two years. It was edited by Mrs. Caroline Gilman.

South-Western Monthly, The, a Journal Devoted to Literature and Science, Education, the Mechanic Arts and Agriculture, published at Nashville in 1852.

Una, The, a monthly published in 1853 and 1854 at Providence, Rhode Island and in 1855 at Boston. Mrs. Paulina Wright Davis was editor the first two years. In 1855 she was first assisted and then succeeded by Mrs. Caroline Dall.

United States Magazine and Democratic Review, The (1837–1851); *The Democratic Review* (1852); *The United States Review* (1853–1855); *The United States Democratic Review* (1856–1859), published monthly (1837–1856; July 1857–1858); weekly (January–June 1857); in Washington (1837–1840); in New York (1841–1859).

Universalist and Ladies' Repository, The, published in Boston from 1832 to 1873. It was usually edited by Universalist clergymen. From 1832 to 1838 it was known as *The Universalist;* after 1843 its full title was, *Ladies' Repository: A Universalist Monthly Magazine for the Home Circle.*

Wellman's Literary Miscellany, a monthly published in Detroit from July 1849 to August 1854 for a dollar a year. The title was changed in March 1851 to *Monthly Literary Miscellany: a Compendium of Literary, Philosophical and Religious Knowledge;* Daniel F. Quimby became editor; Beecher and Quimby publishers.

Western Literary Cabinet, a monthly edited in 1853 and 1854 by Mrs. Electra M. Sheldon and published in Detroit, Michigan by D. F. Quimby & Co. in 1853 and by George E. Pomeroy & Co. in 1854. The subscription was a dollar a year.

Western Casket, The, a monthly edited and published at St. Louis, Missouri by the Reverend S. A. Hodgman from December 1850 through 1853, for a dollar a year. Volume I (1850) was known as *The Presbyterian Casket of Sacred and Polite Literature;* volume III as *The Casket, Devoted to Religion and Literature.* All volumes were called *The Western Casket.*

Western Journal of Agriculture, Manufacture, Mechanic Arts, Internal Improvement, Commerce and General Literature, The, a monthly published in St. Louis, Missouri from 1848 through April 1853. M. Traver was editor. He had as co-editors F. Rick (1849–1852), and H. Cobb (October 1852–1853).

Western Literary Journal and Monthly Review, The, was edited by William D. Gallagher and published by Smith and Day at Cincinnati from June to November, inclusive, 1836. It was later merged with the *Western Monthly Magazine* to form *Western Monthly Magazine and Literary Journal.*

Western Literary Magazine and Journal of Education, Science, Arts and Morals, The, edited by George Brewster and published at Columbus in 1851 and at Cleveland in 1854. Except for one paragraph in the "Preface," the two are alike. They are the same "Miscellany."

Western Literary Messenger, The, a Family Magazine of Literature, Science, Art, Morality and General Intelligence, published from August 1841 through 1857 at Buffalo, New York. Jesse Clement was editor.

Western Magazine and Review, The (May–July 1827), *The Western Monthly Review* (August 1827–June 1830), a monthly published at the close of every month at Cincinnati and conducted by Timothy Flint. The cost was $3.00 a year if paid in advance; $4.00 if paid semi-annually.

Western Messenger, The, Devoted to Religion and Literature, a monthly published at Cincinnati (1835–1836, 1839–1841) and at Louisville (1836–1839). It was begun as the organ of the Unitarian Church and was at one time published by the Western Unitarian Association (1836–1837). Editors included Ephraim Peabody (June 1835–February 1836), James Freeman Clark (April 1836–through 1839) and William H. Channing (May 1839–April 1841).

Western Miscellany, a monthly edited and published at Dayton, Ohio, by B. F. Ellis from July 1848 to June 1849.

Western Monthly Magazine, The. The titles and places of publication were: *The Illinois Monthly Magazine,* October 1830–September 1832 (Vandalia, Illinois, 1830–1831, then at Cincinnati); *The Western Monthly Magazine, a Continuation of the Illinois Monthly Magazine,* 1833–1835 (Cincinnati); *The Western Monthly Magazine,* 1836 (Cincinnati); *The Western Monthly Magazine and Literary Journal,* 1837 (Louisville). James Hall was editor from 1830 to June 1836.

Western Plow Boy, devoted to Agriculture and the Agriculturist, was edited by R. D. Turner and J. P. Jenks at Fort Wayne, Indiana. It was published bi-monthly during January, February and March, 1853.

Since the aim of this study has been to winnow ideas on education from the wealth of other material in magazines for ladies and literary journals from 1830 to 1860 and to set these ideas in their historic and educational setting, the secondary sources deal with four kinds of material: 1. The magazines; 2. Educational movements in the period 1830–1860; 3. Historic and literary material about these decades; 4. Biographical accounts of editors, writers, and leaders of movements. The secondary sources have, therefore, been grouped under these four topics.

MATERIAL ABOUT MAGAZINES

The outstanding book on this subject is Frank Luther Mott's *A History of American Magazines* (3 volumes, Cambridge, Massachusetts, Harvard University Press, 1938–1939). Vol. I deals with the magazines 1741–1850; vol. II, 1850–1865. Bertha Monica Stearns has written a series of articles on magazines for ladies. These include: "Early New England Magazines for Ladies" in *The New England Quarterly*, vol. II, no. 3, 1929, pp. 420–457; "New England Magazines for Ladies 1830–1860" in *The New England Quarterly*, vol. III, no. 4, 1930, pp. 627–656; "Early Philadelphia Magazines for Ladies" in *The Pennsylvania Magazine of History and Biography*, vol. LXIV, no. 4, October 1940, pp. 479–491; "Philadelphia Magazines for Ladies: 1830–1860" in *The Pennsylvania Magazine of History and Biography*, vol. LXIX, no. 3, July 1945, pp. 207–219; "Reform Periodicals and Female Reformers" in *American Historical Review*, vol. XXXVII, no. 4, July 1932, pp. 678–699; "Southern Magazines for Ladies (1819–1860)" in *The South Atlantic Quarterly*, vol. XXXI, no. 1, January 1932, pp. 70–87; "Early Western Magazines for Ladies" in *The Mississippi Valley Historical Review*, vol. XVIII, no. 5, December 1931, pp. 319–350. William B. Cairns "Magazines, Annuals and Gift Books," in *The Cambridge History of American Literature* (New York, G. P. Putnam's Sons, 4 volumes) Book II, Chapter XX, pp. 160 ff. The standard guide for the magazine holdings of the libraries is the *Union List of Serials in Libraries of the United States and Canada*, edited by Winifred Gregory (New York, The H. H. Wilson Company, 1945).

EDUCATION

In the following books is material about the educational movements from 1830 to 1860.

William C. Bagley, *A Century of the Universal School* (New York, The Macmillan Company, 1937, xiv, 185 pp.).

Henry Barnard, *Papers for the Teacher,* republished from *Barnard's American Journal of Education* (New York, F. C. Brownell, 1860, 434 pp.).

Mrs. I. M. E. Blandin, *History of Higher Education of Women in the South to 1860* (New York and Washington, The Neale Publishing Company, 1909, 328 pp.).

Rachel L. Bodley, *Introductory Lecture Delivered at the Opening of the Twenty-Sixth Annual Session of the Woman's Medical College of Pennsylvania,* October 7, 1875 (Philadelphia, Grant, Faries and Rodgers, 1875, 16 pp.).

Robert Wayne Clark, *The Genesis of the Philadelphia High School for Girls* (Philadelphia, D. Ed. Thesis Temple University, 1938, 150 pp.).

Ellwood P. Cubberley, *Public Education in the United States* (Boston, Houghton Mifflin Company, 1934, xviii, 782 pp.).

Ellwood P. Cubberley, *The History of Education* (Boston, Houghton Mifflin Company, 1920, xxiv, 849 pp.).

Merle Curti, *The Social Ideas of American Educators* (Part X of the *Report of the Commission on the Social Studies*) (New York, Charles Scribner's Sons, 1935, xi, 613 pp.).

Edwin Grant Dexter, *History of Education in the United States* (New York, Macmillan, 1904, ix, 656 pp.).

Frederick Eby and Charles Flinn Arrowood, *The Development of Modern Education* (New York, Prentice-Hall, Inc., 1934, xxiv, 922 pp.).

Willard S. Elsbree, *The American Teacher* (New York, American Book Company, 1939, ix, 566 pp.).

Willystine Goodsell, *Education of Women, Its Social Background and Problems* (New York, Macmillan, 1923, xii, 378 pp.).

E. D. Grizell, *Origin and Development of the High School in New*

England before 1865 (New York, The Macmillan Company, 1923, xv, 428 pp.).

I. L. Kandel, *History of Secondary Education, A Study in the Development of Liberal Education* (Boston, Houghton Mifflin Company, 1930, xvii, 577 pp.).

Edgar W. Knight, *Education in the United States,* Second Revised Edition (Boston, Ginn and Company, 1941, xvi, 669, xii).

———— "A Century of Teacher Education" in *The Educational Forum,* vol. IX, no. 2, January 1945, pp. 149–161.

Paul Monroe, *A Cyclopedia of Education* (New York, The Macmillan Company, 1910–1913, 5 volumes).

———— *Founding of the American Public School System* (New York, The Macmillan Company, 1940, xiv, 520 pp.).

———— *A Text-Book in the History of Education* (New York, The Macmillan Company, 1911, xxiii, 772 pp.).

James Mulhern, *A History of Secondary Education in Pennsylvania,* (Philadelphia, published by the author, 1933, xv, 714 pp.).

Stuart G. Noble, *A History of American Education* (New York, Farrar and Rinehart, Inc., 1938, xv, 440 pp.).

L. B. Pekin, *Coeducation in Its Historical and Theoretical Setting* (London, The Hogarth Press, 1939, 208 pp.).

Edward H. Reisner, *The Evolution of the Common School* (New York, The Macmillan Company, 1930, x, 590 pp.).

———— *Nationalism and Education Since 1789* (New York, The Macmillan Company, 1929, xiii, 575 pp.).

George P. Schmidt, "Intellectual Crosscurrents in American Colleges, 1825–1855" in *American Historical Review,* volume XLII, no. 1, October 1936, pp. 46–67.

Calvin E. Stowe, *Common Schools and Teacher Seminaries* (Boston, March, Capen, Lyon and Webb, 126 pp.).

Richard Thursfield, *Henry Barnard's American Journal of Education* (Baltimore: Johns Hopkins University Press, 1946, 359 pp.).

James Pyle Wickersham, *History of Education in Pennsylvania* (Lancaster, 1886, 683 pp.).

Thomas Woody, *A History of Women's Education in the United
States* (New York and Lancaster, Pa., The Science Press, 1929,
2 vols.).

Recently there have been a number of magazine articles and books
which re-evaluate education for the layman. The controversy about
progressive schools has been carried to the popular periodicals. William Owen has presented "My Case Against Progressive Education"
in *The Saturday Evening Post,* vol. 217, no. 52, June 23, 1945, pp.
14 ff. and Sidney Hook has presented "The Case for Progressive
Education" in *The Saturday Evening Post,* vol. 217, no. 53, June
30, 1945, pp. 28 ff. James L. Mursell has given a negative answer
to the question "Is Progressive Education Through" in *American
Mercury,* vol. LX, no. 258, July 1945, pp. 706–712.

The whole question of general versus scientific education seems
constantly to be discussed. *General Education in a Free Society, Report of the Harvard Committee* (Cambridge, Massachusetts, Harvard University Press, 1945, xix, 267 pp.) is a significant book on
the value of general education. Herman Harrell Horne has written
on "Three Competing Philosophies of Education" in *The Educational Forum,* vol. IX, no. 2, January 1945, pp. 133 ff. Jacques Bar-
zun in his provocative book, *Teacher in America* (Boston, Little
Brown, 1945, 321 pp.) makes, among other things, a good case for
general education. So do Wallace B. Donham, *Education for Responsible Living* (Cambridge, Massachusetts, Harvard University
Press, 1945, xii, 309 pp.) and an anonymous writer in "Letter to a
Seventeen Year Old Son" in *Harper's Magazine,* vol. 191, no. 1143,
August 1945, pp. 167–174. In "Why I Read the Bible" (in *The
Atlantic,* September 1945, pp. 63–66) Lt. Com. C. Leslie Glenn
obliquely makes a case for scientific training as opposed to a liberal
education. Paul R. Mort, *The Inglis Lecture, 1943: Secondary Education as Public Policy* (Cambridge, Massachusetts, Harvard University Press, 1943, 85 pp.) has an interesting discussion of the
relation between the quality of teaching and teachers' salaries. These
articles and books are mentioned, not that they form a complete list,
but that they suggest discussions today parallel to those of a century
ago.

Since this study deals primarily with the play of ideas, there are several books which have been invaluable. First, is Merle Curti, *The Growth of American Thought* (New York, Harper and Brothers Publishers, 1943, xx, 848 pp.). The others are: Vernon Louis Parrington, *Main Currents in American Thought, An Interpretation of American Literature from the Beginnings to 1920* (New York, Harcourt, Brace and Company, 1930, xvii, 428 pp.); Willard Thorp, Merle Curti and Carlos Baker, *American Issues* (Philadelphia, J. B. Lippincott, 1941, 2 volumes) especially volume I, *The Social Record;* Arthur Alphonse Ekirch, Jr., *The Idea of Progress in America 1815–1860* (New York, Columbia University Press, 1944, 305 pp.) and Arthur Meier Schlesinger, *New Viewpoints in American History* (New York, The Macmillan Company, 1928, x, 299 pp.) especially chapter VI, "The Role of Women in American History"; Ralph Henry Gabriel, *The Course of American Democratic Thought, and Intellectual History since 1815* (New York, The Ronald Press Company, 1940, xi, 452 pp.). Although there is no relation to content, Alfred North Whitehead's *Adventure of Ideas* (New York, The Macmillan Company, 1933, ix, 392 pp.) has been most helpful.

Among the histories of the United States, the two which have been most useful are the three volumes of *A History of American Life,* edited by Arthur M. Schlesinger and Dixon Ryan Fox (New York, The Macmillan Company, 1927–1945, XII volumes),—volume V, *The Completion of Independence,* 1790–1830 by John Allen Krout and Dixon Ryan Fox (New York, The Macmillan Company, 1944, xxii, 487 pp.), volume VI, *The Rise of the Common Man, 1830*–1850 by Carl Russell Fish (New York, The Macmillan Company, 1941, xix, 391 pp.), and volume VII, *The Irrepressible Conflict, 1850–1865,* by Arthur Charles Cole (New York, The Macmillan Company, 1943, xii, 468 pp.); and John Bach McMaster, *A History of the People of the United States, from the Revolution to the Civil War* (New York, D. Appleton and Company, 1906–1928, 7 volumes), especially volume VI, 1830–1842, volume VII, 1841–1850 and volume VIII, 1850–1861. Others which have been useful include: Charles A. and Mary R. Beard, *The Rise of American Civilization* (New York, The Macmillan Company, 1927–1939, 3 volumes)— volume I deals with this period; Edward Channing, *History of the*

United States (New York, The Macmillan Company, 6 volumes, 1909–1923) volumes V and VI; James Ford Rhodes, *History of the United States from the Compromise of 1850* (New York, The Macmillan Company, 7 volumes, 1893–1906) especially volume I; several volumes in *The Chronicles of America Series,* edited by Allen Johnson (New Haven, Connecticut, Yale University Press, 1918–1921, 50 volumes) as volume 26, Emerson Hough, *The Passing of the Frontier* (1921, 181 pp.), volume 27, William E. Dodd, *The Cotton Kingdom* (1921, 161 pp.), Jesse Macy, *The Anti-Slavery Crusade* (1921, 245 pp.); and several volumes of *The American Nation, A History,* edited by A. B. Hart (Harper and Brothers, New York, 1906, 27 volumes), as volume 15, William MacDonald, *Jacksonian Democracy 1829–1837* (1906, xiv, 345 pp.); volume 17, George Pierce Garrison, *Westward Extension* (1906, xiv, 366 pp.); volume 18, Theodore Clarke Smith, *Parties and Slavery 1850–1859* (1906, xvi, 341 pp.); and volume 19, French Ensor Chadwick, *Causes of the Civil War* (1906, xiv, 372 pp.). *Appleton's Cyclopaedia of American History* (New York, D. Appleton and Company, 1888, 7 volumes) and *The Encyclopaedia Britannica* (eleventh edition [29 volumes] or earlier editions) have been useful. Such local histories as the *History of the State of New York,* A. C. Flick, editor (New York, Columbia University Press, 1934, 10 volumes); the *Annals of Philadelphia* by John Fanning Watson (Philadelphia, E. S. Stuart, 1877, 3 volumes) and the *History of Philadelphia, 1609–1884,* by John Thomas Scharf and Thompson Westcott (Philadelphia, L. H. Everts and Company, 1884, 2 volumes) have been helpful. It was necessary to consult reference books, published nearly a century ago, as John J. Anderson, *Pictorial History of United States* (New York, Clark and Maynard, 1867, 363 pp.) and J. H. French, *Gazeteer of State of New York* (Syracuse, New York, Clark and Maynard, 1860, 752 pp.).

Within recent years a number of social and literary histories have been published. Alice Felt Tyler, *Freedom's Ferment, Phases of American Social History to 1860* (Minneapolis, The University of Minnesota Press, 1944, x, 608 pp.) and Arthur M. Schlesinger, Jr., *The Age of Jackson* (Boston, Little, Brown and Company, 1945, 577 pp.) are valuable. Other social and literary histories include: two books by Fred Lewis Pattee, *The First Century of American Literature* (New York, D. Appleton-Century Company, 1940, vii

613 pp.) and *The Feminine Fifties* (New York, D. Appleton-Century Company, 1940, xii, 339 pp.); Meade Minnigerode, *The Fabulous Forties, 1840–1850* (New York, G. P. Putnam's Sons, 1924, xvi, 345 pp.); *The Cambridge History of Literature* (New York, G. P. Putnam's Sons, 1917–1921, 4 volumes); Van Wyck Brooks, *The Flowering of New England* (New York, E. P. Dutton, 1936, 550 pp.) and *The World of Washington Irving* (New York, E. P. Dutton, 1944, 495 pp.); Ellis Paxson Oberholtzer, *The Literary History of Philadelphia* (Philadelphia, Jacobs, 1906, 433 pp.); Struthers Burt, *Philadelphia, Holy Experiment* (Garden City, New York, Doubleday, 1945, 396 pp.); Gilbert Seldes, *The Stammering Century* (New York, The John Day Company, 1928, xviii, 474 pp.); E. Douglas Branch, *The Sentimental Years, 1836–1860* (New York, D. Appleton-Century Company, 1934, xii, 432 pp.); Olga Elizabeth Winslow, "Books for the Lady Reader, 1820–1860" in *Romanticism in America* (Baltimore, Johns Hopkins University Press, 1940, 202 pp.); Thelma M. Smith, "Feminism in Philadelphia" in *The Pennsylvania Magazine of History and Biography,* volume LXVIII, number 23, July 1944, pp. 243–268; Jeanette P. Nichols, "The Nurture of Feminism in the United States" in *The Harvard Educational Review,* volume XI, number 3, May 1941, pp. 347–358.

BIOGRAPHY

The *Dictionary of American Biography,* edited by Allen Johnson and Dumas Malone (New York, The Macmillan Company, 20 volumes, 1928–1940) and *Appleton's Cyclopaedia and American Biography* (New York, D. Appleton, 1887–1900, 7 volumes) have biographical material. *The History of Woman's Suffrage,* by Elizabeth Cady Stanton, Susan B. Anthony and others (Rochester, New York, Mann, 4 volumes, 1881–1902) has detailed information about most of the women who were prominent in this period. *Pioneers of Women's Education in the United States,* by Willystine Goodsell (New York, McGraw, Hill Company, 1931, vii, 311 pp.) has excellent material on Mary Lyon, Emma Willard and Catharine Beecher.

In addition, the following biographical material has been helpful. The material is listed, under the person about whom it is written.

Susan B. Anthony—Rheta Childe Dorr, *Susan B. Anthony, the Woman Who Changed the Mind of a Nation* (New York, Frederick A. Stokes Co., 1928, 367 pp.).

CATHARINE E. BEECHER—Mae Elizabeth Harveson, *Catharine Esther Beecher, a Pioneer Educator* (Philadelphia, Science Press, 1932, 295 pp.).

AMELIA BLOOMER—Amelia Bloomer, "History of the Lily," a newspaper clipping from the "Woman's Kingdom" of the Chicago *Interocean* in March 1893 on file with copies of *The Lily* at the New York State Library, Albany. There also are letters which Mrs. Bloomer wrote to Mrs. Lillian G. Brown on March 21 and 24, 1893 in which she gave the history of *The Lily* and made comments upon it.

D. C. Bloomer, *Life and Writings of Amelia Bloomer* (Boston, Arena Publishing Company, 1895, 387 pp.).

E. Douglas Branch, "The Lily and the Bloomer" in *Colophon,* Part XII, December 1932, pp. 1–12.

John H. Keatley, "Amelia Bloomer" in *Annals of Iowa,* vol. XII, no. 3, July 1874, pp. 190–194.

John H. Keatley, "Hon. D. C. Bloomer" in *Annals of Iowa,* vol. XII, no. 1, January 1874, pp. 21–24.

SARAH JOSEPHA HALE—Isabelle Webb Entriken, *Sarah Josepha Hale, and Godey's Lady's Book* (Philadelphia, University of Pennsylvania, 1946, vi, 155 pp.).

Ruth Finley, *The Lady of Godey's* (Philadelphia, J. B. Lippincott Company, 1931, 318 pp.).

Eloise Lounsberry, *Saints and Rebels* (New York, Longmans, Green and Company, 1937, 336 pp.) "Sarah Josepha Hale," pp. 223–240.

Lawrence Martin "The Genesis of Godey's Lady's Book" in *The New England Quarterly Review,* vol. 1, no. 1, January 1928, pp. 41–79.

Richardson Wright, *Forgotten Ladies* (Philadelphia, J. B. Lippincott Company, 1928, 307 pp.), "Madonna in Bustle," pp. 187–217.

MARY LYON—Marion Lansing, editor, *Mary Lyon, through Her Letters* (Boston, Massachusetts, Books, Inc., 1937, xiii, 317 pp.).

Arthur Charles Cole, *A Hundred Years of Mount Holyoke College; the Evolution of an Educational Ideal* (New Haven, Yale University Press, 426 pp.).

MRS. LINCOLN PHELPS—Emma Lydia Bolzau, *Almira Hart Lincoln Phelps, Her Life and Work* (Philadelphia, Science Press, 1936, 543 pp.).

ELIZABETH CADY STANTON—Alma Lutz, *Created Equal, a Biography of Elizabeth Cady Stanton* (New York, The John Day Company, 1940, 345 pp.)

    Elizabeth Cady Stanton, *Eighty Years and More, 1815–1897; Reminiscences* (New York, European Publishing Company, 1898, 474 pp.).

    Harriot Stanton Blatch, *A Sketch of the Life of Elizabeth Cady Stanton by Her Daughter* (New York, Harper and Brothers, 1915, 369 pp.).

    Harriot Stanton Blatch and Theodore Stanton, editors, *Elizabeth Cady Stanton as Revealed in Her Letters, Diary and Reminiscences* (New York, Harper and Brothers, 1922, 2 volumes).

JANE GREY SWISSHELM—Jane Grey Swisshelm, *Half a Century* (Chicago, Jansen, McClurg and Company, second edition, 1880, 363 pp.).

    S. J. Fisher, "Reminiscences of Jane Grey Swisshelm" in *Western Pennsylvania Historical Magazine,* vol. 4, 1921, pp. 165–174.

    Daniel S. B. Johnson, "Minnesota Journalism in the Territorial Period" in *Collections of the Minnesota Historical Society,* vol. X, part I, pp. 247–351 (pp. 344–347 deal with Mrs. Swisshelm).

    Arthur J. Larson, editor, *Crusader and Feminist, Letters of Jane Grey Swisshelm, 1858–1865,* volume II of *Minnesota Historical Society Letters and Documents* (St. Paul, Minnesota Historical Society, 1934, 327 pp.).

    Lester B. Shippee, "Jane Grey Swisshelm, Agitator" in *Mississippi Valley Historical Review,* vol. 7, December 1920, pp. 206–227.

EMMA WILLARD—Alma Lutz, *Emma Willard* (Boston, Houghton Mifflin Company, 1929, 291 pp.).

Index

groes, 119-20; normal schools, 91-100; prevent crime, 118; public, 73-90; women, 32-72, 84-87, 91-104, 121-27

Elmira, 71

Ellet, Mrs., 5, 6, 36

Elsbree, Willard S., 92-93, 155

Embury, Emma C., 145, 146

Emerson, Ralph, 143

Entriken, Isabelle W., 1, 6, 46, 161

Esselen, Christian, 142

European educators, 26, 60, 63, 101, 102, 134

Everett, Edward, 71

Ewer, F. C., 15-16

Family Magazine, 144

Fellenberg, 63, 134

Female Medical College, New England, 124; Pennsylvania, 124-25

Fenelon, 39

"Fern, Fanny," 15

Fish, Carl Russell, 122, 158

Flint, Timothy, 20, 25, 26, 153

Follen, Charles, 53

Fowle, William B., 143

France Littéraire, 16, 17, 144

Frank Leslie's Illustrated Newspaper, 16-18, 51, 74, 75, 117, 144

Frank Leslie's Illustrirte Zeitung, 17, 18, 54, 64, 82, 144

Frank Leslie's New Family Magazine, 111, 114

Franklin Ladies' College, 71

Free Enquirer, 16, 26, 29, 144

free schools, 73 ff.

French Institute, 63-64

Frémont, 19

Friend of Virtue, 11, 110, 113, 144

Froebel, 109, 134

Frontier Monthly, 21, 30, 51, 144

Fuller, Margaret, 16, 143

Gage, Matilda Joslyn, 12

Gallaudet, T. A., 91, 115

Gallagher, William D., 142

German, to preserve German culture, 54; demand for public support of German speaking schools, 89

gift books, 7

Gilman, Caroline, 21, 107, 113, 151

girls, "finishing," 33-35, 58, 67; "finishing schools," 45-47; educated to be wife, 32-35; educated to be mother, 36, 37; educated to marry, 34, 35; curricula, 44-58

Gleason, Frederick, 144

Gleason's Pictorial Review, 29, 70, 81, 117, 144

Godey's Lady's Book, 1-6, 22-25, 33-39, 41, 43, 46-50, 52-56, 60-64, 66-72, 79, 80, 85-87, 93-95, 97-102, 105, 110-13, 116-19, 122-26, 132, 134, 138, 144

Godey, Louis A., 47, 144

Graham, George R., 145

Graham's Magazine, 4-5, 28, 145

Grant, Zilpah P., 44, 47

Greeley, Horace, 78, 88, 125

Grimké, Sarah, 63

Griswold, Rufus W., 145

Groves, Ernest R., 137

Guernsey, Alfred H., 145

Hale, (Miss) Sarah Josepha, 46-47, 67

Hale, (Mrs.) Sarah Josepha, 3-4, 6-7, 21-22, 24-25, 41, 49, 52-54, 66, 68-72, 80, 84-87, 93-100, 106-107, 113, 122-24, 131-32, 135-36, 138, 144-47

Hall, Motte, 45

Hall, Samuel R., 91

Hamilton College, 129

Harper's Monthly Magazine, 15, 20, 22, 26, 29-30, 34, 42, 46, 47, 77, 83, 94, 104, 145

Harrington, Henry F., 105

Hart, John S., 116, 134, 143, 150

Harvard, 128, 129

Hasbrouck, Drs. Lydia Sayer, 61, 80, 123-25, 132, 151

Haswell, J. G., 38

Haüy, Valentine, 114, 117

Henkle, Rev. M. M., 151